I ONCE WAS A PILGRIM

BRIANA GERVAT

For Melissa.

It has always been for Melissa.

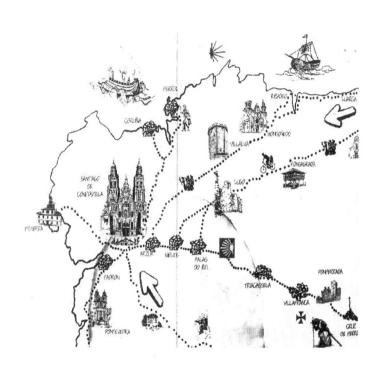

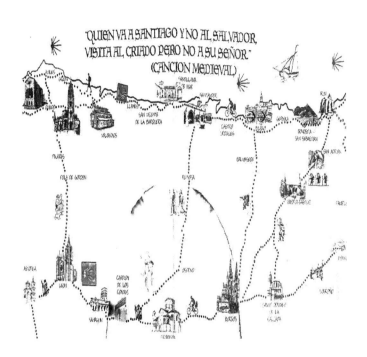

The Chapters

THE POEMS

REMEMBRANCE

IN ISTANBUL

You do not have to be good.
You do not have to walk on your knees
for a hundred miles through the desert repenting.
You only have to let the soft animal of your body
love what it loves.
Tell me about despair, yours, and I will tell you mine.
Meanwhile the world goes on.
Meanwhile the sun and the clear pebbles of the rain
are moving across the landscapes,
over the prairies and the deep trees,
the mountains and the rivers.
Meanwhile the wild geese, high in the clean blue air,
are heading home again.
Whoever you are, no matter how lonely,
the world offers itself to your imagination,
calls to you like the wild geese, harsh and exciting
over and over announcing your place
in the family of things.

Wild Geese
Mary Oliver

pilgrim

noun pil·grim \ ˈpil-grəm \

: one who journeys in foreign lands
: wayfarer
: one who travels to a shrine or holy place as a
devotee

My mother always speaks of time in terms of velocity; how it speeds rather than slows in its progression. And this quickening of time is not graceful, but clumsy, breaking hearts as it passes, stealing thunder, and pulling rugs out from under feet. Unbounded, it cares not for beginnings nor does it care much for ends. My mother may speak of time in this way but for me time only exists in two forms:

There is now and there is never.

There is nothing else.

"What if the world disappoints you?" my mother asked as she turned the faucet on, allowing the water to grow warm. We were having one of our bathroom conversations in which we dance around one another in front of the vanity and speak of all the things that are on our minds and in our hearts. It was one of those rare occasions in which my mother questioned my motives for the journey I was about to undertake.

"What if it doesn't?" I countered with words always spoken by the hopeful- and the stubborn- as I looked into the mirror and plucked from my hair a single gray that told of an age that I was not ready to accept. The years, where had they gone?

"I just want you to be happy," she went on and I gave her that look that only daughters are able to give their mothers.

"Happiness. How boring." I say this because happiness was a word that I allowed only to stand in the shadows of my life and rarely allowed it into the light.

Now it is her turn to give me that look, the look that only mothers can give their daughters. This has been

2

our ongoing battle: her trying to teach me sooner rather than later all that she learned in her life and me resisting her every step of the way. What can I say? I am steadfast in my sadness.

Besides, for years I had denied this happiness, believing in it as much as I believe that the earth is flat. And for me, happiness was not on this island, nor this country for that matter. Here my thoughts become like this place: overcrowded, noisy, restless, always in motion, and never still. Out there, they are free.

And so it is in the days before I depart that I confess to her that I must leave. There are too many things that I have been holding onto for far longer than I should. Perhaps if I were to let go of these things then maybe my sadness might finally give way to the happiness of which she speaks, a happiness as foreign to me as the lands I was about to travel through. But one thing was familiar in all of this:

My happiness does not have roots.

My happiness loves to spread its wings.

"She is going to find her spirit," he pipped from across the deck. It was a Saturday. Three days before my departure.

"What did you say, Moo?" I asked through tears. I had heard what he said but I wanted to hear it from him again: my nephew, my god monster, and the love of my life. And so, I pulled him in close to me, as close as can be.

"You are going to go find your spirit, that is why you are leaving," he said in the voice that echoes, how it echoes in my heart. And then he offered that smile, that mischievous grin that will both get him into trouble and get him out of it.

He had turned five only the month before. Under the warm April sun I wrapped my arms around him, wondering when it was that my arms had grown so small because it could not be so that five years had passed since the day he was born and he was already this big.

Time does this, moving so swiftly that you spend more time in your memories than you do in the present moment, so much so that when asked what

4

time it is, what day it is, what year, you ask only one question in return: What does it matter?

I held him this way, unwilling to let go, and thought that maybe it was not that my spirit had been lost, but I was in search of something: words, ruins, art, adventure. All of me wanted to learn what happens after love. I needed to know why war is continuously waged; and if ever there is such thing as peace. And maybe I had never learned any of these things before. Or maybe I had learned them everywhere, but only in pieces, and it was only now coming together. There was but one thing I knew before departing on this journey:

You find what you seek.

THE BEGINNING BEFORE THE BEGINNING

Some people go to India in search of things they fear may not be found anywhere but there. I just went to visit Kate. For more than a decade Kate, my friend and teammate from college, had been trying to get me to visit her wherever it was that she was living at the time and by now, ten years later, I had run out of reasons not to come. But India was never a place that called my name. I was never drawn to it, never longed for it the way I long for other lands. But I went, nevertheless. I live without regret, except perhaps for having chosen the fourth month of the year as my month of arrival for the sweetness of spring, which had only just begun in New York, is no match for the swelter of the subcontinent in April. Even if I knew, the date of departure would not have changed. In America I could not stay. In the months and years leading up to the presidential election, the chasm that divided Americans from one another had grown to an unbearable width and I feared that so far separated had we become that a middle ground might never be found again. Both a lover and an abhorrent of drama, I left America with the awareness that there is no sense in watching an empire collapse when the world continues to spin just the same.

For me, India was to be a time for me to choose the direction in which it spun: either toward everything I ever hoped for or away from the belief that one day all those dreams might come true. Ever the optimist I chose the former, no longer willing to let anything (or anyone) stand in my way, not even myself. By thirty- six I had lost count of all the things that I entered with hope only to depart with heartbreak so in order to keep my hope- and my heart intact- I entered nothing at all. But I cannot tell you the exact moment at which I shut the door to my heart thinking that this was the only way to protect myself from sadness. It was not sudden, but slow. I feared that if I closed it too fast then forever locked it would stay with neither key nor knob to open it. But to close your heart you must also close your eyes and your eyes, so shuttered and blinded, is no way to see the world

"Pack light," Kate said. "It's starting to get warm." Fool that I am, I listened and boarded the plane in preparation for all the springs that I have ever known. At night, always at night, I entered this land of Bharata Varsha, the air still, the heat rising, and the city asleep.

Over and over again I return to these places of convergence seeking refuge in all that rises in the hope that I, too, shall rise.

In the morning I woke to all that is Delhi: the shrill call of tropical birds, the shouts of monkeys, and a sun that spoke of summer and not of spring. At noon, among mad dogs, I moved from life before India to everything after. Ever the host, Kate arranged for a driver to guide me through the city. At the appointed hour he arrived, standing outside of her apartment in brown slacks and a perfectly pressed, short sleeved buttoned-down shirt. His hair was carefully parted to one side and a smile crept up on the other. With the alacrity of a man who has done this before, he commandeered my bags with one hand and held the door open with the other, summoning me inside the car with a nod of his head and a lopsided grin. Never one to settle for anything less than behind the wheel, it was strange to now be a passenger, without so much as pedals beneath my feet. When the door closed, I was reminded of what a privilege it is to share a car with just one other and no more. For in Delhi resides a population that swells and surges like the waters of coming monsoons. It is a flood of sixteen million people; a madness tempered; a madness unleashed.

The history of Delhi can be peeled back layer-by-layer, century-by-century. It begins with ancient and primal dynasties that gave birth to language and lore. It is then followed by Moghul empires, the rise and fall of British rule, and finally, 'freedom', but it a freedom that is founded upon a caste system where some are still more free than others.

Thousands of years after its founding Delhi continues to be a city crowded with a seemingly endless procession of people. Among them: listless men wearing lunghi and little else, who lay on their sides in whatever shade might be found, their arms draped over their heads, shielding their eyes from the nebulous light, their shoeless black-soled feet exposed to the sun. On every street brazen women swayed in sarees of saffron, crimson, Aurelian, and sage, their skin laced with henna,

10

their torsos bare. More modest women peered out from behind the veils of burkhas, seeing their world through kohl lined eyes. Children walked through traffic carrying the weight of the world in their arms in the form of another child. What ease, what heaviness there was in their burdens. As they stepped between the crowd of cars, their hands out, their eyes unflinching, I wondered when it was that we taught ourselves to look away. And then that familiar thought returned: I could have been born somewhere else, someone else. It is only a question of fate.

The children disappeared from view and still everywhere there was movement, for India is a world in ceaseless motion. Here, life clings to you like the heat as if all of India is breathing, surging, purging, all of it collapsing and expanding in front of your eyes. Even held in the sway are buildings left unfinished, architecture incomplete, and ruins that speak of an unstoppable entropy, a physics divine.

The fragrance of frangipani in full bloom intermingled with the sweet scent of sweet breads that rose with the heat and pungent aromas of incense mingled with the clouded exhaust of Diesel engines. On these streets the eyes, the ears, the nose, the mouth all vie to be the first to sense what is seen, what is heard, and what is tasted. But to attempt to take it all in is to rely on the belief that one breath of air, one sip of water is enough to sustain all of life; an impossibility. Still I closed my eyes. This is how I commit such moments to memory. A horn blared, issued from a bus so full that even the driver was barely visible behind the soot stained windshield. It was a noise that said you are here; you are in India. *Surrender. Surrender. Surrender.*

We drove on through the delirium of rising heat and fervor. The hour was well before noon and still the temperatures crested over one hundred degrees. Before

11

the sun was at its zenith I attempted to walk through the throngs of the crowd of Masjid-i Jahān-Numā. Also known as the *Jama Masjid*, this mosque was built by Mughal emperor Shah Jahan, the man also responsible for the construction of the Taj Mahal. Completed in 1656, it stands elevated on a porch of sandstone, rising red above the earth, and, as its name implies, it is a mosque commanding a view of the world. Three centuries later it is still one of the largest mosques in all of India.

Only once before had I entered a mosque, but it was smaller and I did not take the time then to admire what was now before me: ornate Moghul architecture of ribs and vaults, half domes and courtyards, and the layers of black and white marble meant to mirror prayer mats.

The fluted minarets towered above the seven arched entranceways that faced west towards Mecca. From their spires is issued the adhan, the Muslim call to prayer. In Arabic these minarets are also called *monar* or *monara*, a place of fire and light and it was easy to see how both believers and nonbelievers alike might be drawn to this place as a moth to a flame.

Here the air was so thick with heat and history that it resisted any and all ability to move forward and so I stood as still as can be in a mosque as old as the country from where I came, In the time between prayers, most visitors were silent, even the children who played in the recesses of the mosque. With bare feet I walked in and out of the shade and shadows of a history so dense and so deep that it might never be known, at least not for a traveler encountering its mysteries for the first time. And so, on the surface I remained, barely scratching it, unable to go below.

When the heat began to remind my feet that they were no match for one another I left the mosque with a hunger not just for food, but for more of Delhi, for India, for life. But eat we must, and my driver and I went to a small restaurant on a small street in the middle of the madness. Imagining that this is where he takes all of Kate's foreign guests, he ordered not from the menu, but from memory and soon steaming dishes of Aloo Gobi, butter Chicken, and Vindaloo arrived at our table. We sat across from one another in silence, not because there was nothing to say, but because all that needed to be said was expressed in the food before us. A 'vegetarian' before leaving I quickly realized that this life without meat was not to last.

As the sun began to fall behind Delhi, casting the city in shadows of its ebbing light, Kate and I met for an early dinner where she introduced me to all the food that she loves in India. By this meal I had fallen in love with naan, be it garlic, butter, or garlic butter, which we shared along with an arugula salad with leaves of fresh mint and seeds of pomegranate that burst on our tongues. Also, on the table was yellow lentil daal, and smaller plates full of food of unpronounceable names and flavors that begged more to be eaten than described. After, we returned to her apartment with the day ending as noisily as it began; a constant hum, a stirring that never stills.

When the weekend arrived, I went with Kate and her friends on a cycling tour through the streets of Old Delhi. Our guide for the day was named Savvy. Tall and lean, he wore a *dastaar*, a turban, upon his head, identifying him as a Sikh. It was yellow, symbolic of happiness and joy; the perfect color for a man whose smile never left his face. So excited was he to show us his city that he made it easy to forget the pandemonium we were about to pedal into; a chaos to which there is no comparison. Even after having learned how to drive in New York, I hesitated to merge into this world that was at once a menagerie and a melee of motorbikes,

13

rickshaws, and taxis vying for an open space where there was none. The old city was more congested than the new; crowded as much with the past as it was the present. How we did not get lost, I do not know, for my heart and my head were dizzy just at the sight of it all.

Everywhere there were carts drawn by horses, oxen, and the hands of men. On their wooden slabs rested an abundance of papayas, watermelons, and limes cut open to reveal the life within. Their rinds were strewn on the ground to be grazed on by sacred cows, both swollen and sunken, and wild dogs that will never know what it means to be tame.

In the maze and haze of Old Delhi we stopped and climbed to the top of a roof to gaze down upon the spice market. On the ground below bushels of chili peppers, dried and bright red, stood side by side with blocks of pink salt, as nuts and legumes spilled forth from darkened stalls. In a roar of sounds and flash of colors it was not difficult to see why empires rose and fell in search of these riches; for these spices I would brave the Cabo das Tormentas, for them I would sail to the ends of the world.

To escape from the inescapable sun, we climbed down the stairs and back onto our bikes to discover more of Delhi. Eventually the boulevards broadened, and the streets were overrun with the roots of banyan trees, their branches dangling with vines and monkeys. This is the quarter where the British lived during their "colonial folly" and even after sixty years of independence it remains a world apart. Under a sprawling canopy of long gray limbs and dark green leaves, we stopped for chai. Holding the small glass in both of my hands, I brought it to my nose and then my lips. Slowly I sipped from the glass, the tea as sweet and hot as the day. It tasted of cardamom and cloves, pepper and ginger. Leaning against a wall, I breathed in deeply from this day.

14

Knowing that the brevity of my stay here would not allow any further passage into this world still I clung to this breath, attaching all other breaths to this moment. I drank from this cup. It was empty and it was full.

Since I was partaking in 'India Light', Kate arranged for a car to take me to all the destinations in the Golden Triangle; that trifecta of tourism that does not allow one to stray far from the beaten path. Only in India for so short a time, I was to be a tourist and nothing more. The driver arrived at dawn when Delhi shimmers in an incandescent light. We drove south out of the city through smog, visible in all directions lightening the day but not brightening it. As we taxied down the highway, he pointed out all of the places that may never make it onto a list of ultimate tourist destinations: another new apartment building meant to house the expanding population of Delhi, roads that ended just meters from where they began, and sites of terrible accidents involving cars, buses, tractor trailers and, even once, a plane, which still lays where it landed; a relic of how anything can happen in India, anything at all.

In the ever-rising heat we arrived in Agra. On a dusty and crowded corner, we picked up N.C., my guide for the day. He was waiting in the shade of a banyan tree in front of an overturned white van, a cow ambling in its wreckage. He smiled warmly as he opened the door. N.C. was a man of about fifty. The years had painted his hair and beard shades and shadows of grey and white, replacing the black it once was. He carried with him the quiet confidence of a man who enjoys what he does and knows that he does it well.

To get to the Taj Mahal we weaved our way through cows and tuk-tuks and past smiling tourists going in the opposite direction. Parking outside of the complex, we slowly made our way towards the entrance, which was guarded by police and armed forces holding guns as casually as they were conversations. For years the Taj Mahal has been under a near constant threat of terrorism, which shows that the world, no matter where, is in constant danger of destroying itself. With ease we walked past these men and through each of the security checkpoints. The day was a holy one and our entrance was free.

Once inside, and impatient New Yorker that I am, I wanted to walk faster to see the Taj Mahal faster, but N.C. knew better than this and he steadied his steps, allowing only the gate to come into view. Did he not know that I had waited my whole life just for this? I think he did for as my steps quickened, his grew slower until we stood just outside of the entrance. Here, Arabic words inscribed in marble climb up the gates, growing larger as the building grows taller. The inscription is an invitation to the world that awaits those who have died, it is an invitation to paradise.

N.C. stood for a moment in silence and then motioned for us to move through the portico. That was when I stopped; that was when all except for this moment ceased to exist. Before me stood the reflecting pool, its waters green and still in the morning light. The Cyprus trees on either side were perfectly pruned and evenly spaced, symbolic of life and death. Standing alone in the distance the mausoleum rose white against the pale blue sky. Despite its apparent solidness, there was a softness to the Taj Mahal that weakened my knees and unsteadied my steps, so much so that I almost fell to the

16

ground and wept. But I held back in fear of what these tears might reveal: that here was a woman so taken by an inanimate object that it became animate and moved her to weep, or even worse, that I was a crazy white woman unable to contain herself. Little did I know that there was no need to fear such things. They are what make us real. They are what keep us sane.

Collecting myself, we toured the grounds; N.C. walking even more slowly now. It was only later that he revealed that he had been in an accident only a few years before where he was thrown from the back of a motorbike. Now he has metal rods rather than bones in his legs, which makes it more difficult for him to move as quickly as he once did. Together we walked in slow steps and our conversation flowed between the history of this place and the story of his life; both told of love and loss and a longing for something that is no longer there.

Closer, the Taj Mahal became bigger still and I looked back across the grounds and tried to imagine what it would look like if the dreams of Shah Jahan had become a reality: two mausoleums, one white and the other black, reflecting both light and darkness in the pools between. Gazing into the eternal distance I thought to myself that if love was made of marble, then surely this was the greatest love of all.

Near the stairs, still trembling, N.C. offered me his hand. It was the kindest of gestures: offering what is unnecessary and expecting nothing in return. Able bodied I hesitated to take it, as if somehow strength would be lost in this moment and not gained. And then I realized how silly this was and I took his hand in mine. When life offers its kindness, it is better to hold on to it than let it go. Once at the top, but not yet ready to let go I asked:

"N.C., are you a Muslim?" Taking my other hand in his,

he turned towards me and said words that I am not soon to forget:

"First, I am a human being. Second, I am an Indian. And lastly, I am a Hindu." I smiled, as did he, knowing that that first sentence was all that matters, what comes after it rarely does.

We continued to walk and talk, this time at his pace and not mine. Of the place of his birth, the Kashmir, he repeated the words written by Persian poet Amir Khusru: "If there is a paradise upon earth, it is here, it is here, it is here." He spoke of his country not as an Indian, but as if he himself is India. For a moment I was jealous of his home for I have yet to find a paradise of my own. But it is only a fleeting jealously until I remembered where I was: standing in a centuries old wonder of the world and that somehow this, too, was paradise.

At the Taj Mahal we stayed until it grew crowded and then we made our way to the Agra Fort, a walled city where once lived the emperors of the Mughal dynasty. By now N.C and I are old friends and we walked among the grounds of the castle arm in arm. At the end of our day together we made plans that if ever I am to visit India again we will both return to this palace and ride up these ramps on the backs of elephants, as the maharajahs used to do, this time not to conquer the world but to allow ourselves to be conquered by it. It saddened me to say goodbye to N.C., but I knew that I would forever remember his words, his kindness, and the slowness of his steps for the rest of this journey for N.C. had taught me what cannot be forgotten: that we are all human beings.

After Agra, the Amber Fort was explored, as was the Monkey Temple, and the city of Jaipur. In 1876, the entire city of Jaipur was painted pink at the behest of Sawai Ram Singh I in order to welcome the Prince of

Wales. There, everything was indeed pink, even the palace.

Outside of the palace, I leaned against pink walls and watched as a metal smith made copper pans. He sat on his haunches and spun the disc on a lathe. He then heated it over smoldering embers before coating it with tin that looked more like ash than metal. When he saw that the pan was properly coated, he swept the rest of the ash away with a dirty rag before turning the new pan in his hands and making small dents on the surface with a small hammer. When he seemed to be satisfied with his work, he cast the pan aside only to begin work again on another. His movements were so deft and deliberate that I forgot that the world went on beyond us until young men, still teenagers, approached and asked where I was from. When they learned that I was from America they smiled and chanted: "Obama. Obama. Obama." And in the fading afternoon light I was reminded of a hope that is no more. And then the question that now inevitably follows: "Trump?" It was a question that I still did not know the answer to and may never. If I were to be honest, I had left America for this reason among many. For weeks after the election I did not speak to my father, unable to comprehend how he voted as he did, incredulous that the most intelligent man that I have ever known was in support of its opposite. Of course, I could have stayed in America and joined arms in protest, but there is more than one way to resist. Besides, it was important for me to leave my country. For I am a child of history and I know that the present of America is no different than the past of other nations and I was curious to know how the world sees itself through even the most difficult times.

That night, after the setting sun left this pink city aflame in coral, I climbed into the back of a rickshaw to see what becomes of Jaipur in the darkness. The driver was a Hindu man who wore long sleeves and long pants and sandals that barely covered the bottoms of his feet. For an hour, maybe two, we toured the streets of his city. On the way back to the hostel, he turned down a road in which we seemed to be the only vehicle traveling in the opposite direction of all others. I laughed as I leaned in to ask:

"Sir, are we driving the wrong way down a one-way street?"

And maybe, long used to these wild and reckless roads that make even thunder road look tame, he took his eyes off the road or maybe he kept them forward. But whichever way he faced he said the words that were to define the rest of my journey:

"This is India, Madam. Nothing is impossible."

And he was right. This was indeed India and nothing, not one thing, was impossible.

After leaving him to the night I climbed to the roof of the hostel where there is a restaurant open to all the stars visible in the sky above Jaipur. On this moonless night a man softly plucked the strings of his guitar. He smiled as I passed and began to sing a melody as melancholy as it was bright. I knew not whether he sang of love or loss, nor did it matter. For dinner, I sat near his stage: alone, but never lonely. Somehow, while traveling, these words lose their meanings. Alone means nothing. Lonely, even less.

Before me was a dish of *chhole*, a chickpea curry as hot as the night and as delightful too. This meal, like all others alone, was a solitary celebration, a reflection upon all that has been and anticipation of all that will be, but this was only the beginning of my journey. It was only the beginning. Long after the last of the spice left my lips and the last of his song escaped from his, the

20

night fell silent and still and sleep came filling the city with dreams.

From Rajasthan I flew to Varanasi, landing in the early hours of a city immersed in chaos as much as it was in calm. Here the dust never settled but rose in the air as dry and dense as the heat. Varanasi is one of the most ancient and holy cities for Hindus. It is the home of Lord Shiva, creator, protector, and transformer of the universe. The Ganges River courses southeast through the city. It is the third largest river in the world, and it flows east some 2,700 kilometers from the western Himalayas to where it empties into the Bay of Bengal. While born of myths and legends, the river plays a vital role in the daily lives of the residents of Varanasi for, like Shiva, its waters are the source of birth, life and even death.

Once in the rickshaw, I did as the drivers do and wrapped a scarf around my head loose enough to see, but tight enough to offer what protection it can. We weaved from one side of the road to the other; if there were lines, they were lost in the dust. Dropped amid the throngs of humanity that heaved and pulsated on every corner, I did not know where I was. There were no street signs. Even if there were, would it matter? I could not speak Hindi, let alone read it. Eventually I found where it was I was meant to stay and stubborn or foolish that I am, the heat knows better than to differentiate between the two, I walked to the famed Ganges River.

On that late April morning the temperature stood suspended over one hundred degrees; the heat and humidity clinging to one another, neither willing to surrender its grasp. The city of Varanasi is like a maze with streets so narrow that even with so small a stature I was able to reach from one side to the other, touching the bricks that have offered shelter and shade for thousands of years. To get to the river was to walk through these narrow passageways before emerging onto one of the many ghats of the city.

Under the unforgiving sun, water swept past, carrying with it all that is holy and unholy in its flood. A cow waded into the river as children swam and splashed one another in the rushing tides and their mothers beat sheets and shirts along the embankment. The day grew hot, too hot to breathe and I returned to my hostel to hide from the sun. Soon the world would grow dark and I would return to the river in time for Aarti, the ritual performed every evening in Varanasi giving thanks to the goddess Gange.

At sundown crowds gathered to watch the ceremony. They sit on the steps of the ghat or in small boats that float close to the shore as children jump in and out of the darkened waters. Along the river lamps and lanterns were lit and the chants of pandits rose above the dancing light. The heat rose too, unabated by the darkness. For more than an hour, cymbals were rung, and small offerings were made to the river. In silence and awe I inched closer to the edge of my seat as did the woman next to me. She had as many years before her as there were behind. A crimson shawl draped across her shoulders, matching the *bindi* in the middle of her wrinkled forehead. Every now and again, we smiled at one another, but never exchanged a word.

For the entirety of the ceremony Saddhus, holy men, came and went from the crowds. Prayer beads were strung from their necks and their hair, plated with dreadlocks, was wrapped in tight buns at the tops of their

22

heads. Their faces were painted orange and white and their expressions did not stray far from the muted bemusement of the pageantry before them, of which they were an integral part. Watching them I almost forget that I, too, am a pilgrim, here to bear testament to all that is seen. Long after the ceremony ended, I fell asleep dreaming of Shiva, dreaming of Maa.

When it was still dark, a noise awakened me from sleep. I rose from my single bed to glance out of the window. Below a parade of pious men shambled through the narrow alley, chanting the chants of what gods they worship as they walked to the river. Some were dressed in saffron robes and carried sticks that they leaned on with each step. Others held drums and tambourines, marching to their beat as they shuffled through the streets. Curious, I dressed and followed them to the Ganga to witness what becomes of light when it travels. Tinged pink, the river reflected wisps of apricot from the clouds above. On the edge of the ghat a man dressed only in lunghi sat cross legged and played his flute, charming the sun from its slumber. Soon it rose like a snake from the east, ending the night and beginning the dawn.

Still early, I returned to the hostel for a small breakfast of fruit and tea. The hostel was run by a young American woman who used to work with Kate at the American Embassy School. She left her post because she felt that it sheltered her from the rest of India. And so, alongside of men and women from Varanasi who cared deeply for their home and their community, she founded a school for children who sometimes lived in houses, but more often lived on the streets of this sacred city.

Wanting to know more of life in India beyond being a tourist I went with one of these men to visit children and their families who lived on the Ganges. When both the sun and the heat were at their highest, I rode on the back of his motorcycle without a helmet through the alleys and unpaved roads of Varanasi, hanging on tightly as we passed cows, wild dogs, women in burkas, shirtless men, and barefoot children. Again, I wrapped my scarf around my face to protect myself not from the wind, but from the dirt that rose from the ground and lingered in the air coating everything in soot and black dust. With the dexterity of someone who knew not the meaning of an open road, we dodged in and out of the already crowded and confined spaces of labyrinthine alleys so narrow that they seemed impossible to pass and yet somehow, we made it through. My grip tightened as we weaved in and out of harm's way, dodging a chicken there, a chai wala there. Eventually, I learned that it was my grip and my grip alone that needed to be loosened.

Before long, we arrived at a place where the Ganges is barely a trickle and what little water that there is, is impeded by plastics and pollution. Along the southern shore of the river we walked past homes that were no more than makeshift tents made of cardboard, tarpaulin, and sometimes sheet metal, or simply the bridge that spanned overhead. He had come to bring medicine and food to the people who lived here. They smiled when they saw him. Perhaps because they knew he saw them too.

At first I remained silent, uncertain what to say or how to act when confronted by so much humanity, but this silence lasted only until I felt a gentle tug on my hand and then another and before I knew it I was surrounded by children, covered in sand and little else. Then I became a tree, not because I was rooted and could not move, but because the children began to climb the branches of my arms and legs before finally coming to rest on my shoulders and for the smallest among them: the top of my head. Their ages were no different than that of my nieces and nephews. How could it be that they lived worlds apart? But knowing that the joy of children is often no different in one part of the world than another, I threw them each in the air again and again as they shrieked with laughter. How light they were. How heavy this is. And while this may have been poverty unabashed this, too, was life unrestricted and this, more than any river, more than any mosque, more than any meal was why I was a pilgrim; to be reminded over and over again that to accept the world for anything less than what it is, is to strip from it its meaning and its magic. We stayed for the whole afternoon, taking our leave only when the light changed from a bright blue to a muted grey.

When the sun escaped from the day taking none of its heat with it, I went down to the river to witness the burning of bodies in the Ganga. In the hopes of achieving moksha, the Hindu belief in which when you die you are finally released from the cycle of rebirth, men prepare the dead for their final ritual, anointing the bodies with incense before laying them in the pyre. This fire burns day and night, the smoke rising, the embers glowing orange and bright. Bells clang in the darkness as the dead are ushered from this world to the next.

A young man, a Dalit by caste, considered an untouchable, sat down beside me. He wore a charcoal t-shirt, a pair of faded blue jeans, and sneakers; the laces loose and dirty, but his soles were clean. His hair was long or at least longer than the beard that he was trying to grow, which was no more than a few stray patches of hair, barely a stubble, barely a shadow that would ever see five o'clock. Handsome and gregarious, he struck up a conversation by offering a cup of tea, which I took reluctantly knowing there was a chance that I was gazing out into the source from which it is made. Assuring me that it was not, he also tried to assuage my fears by

25

proclaiming that it was safe to drink from the Ganga, citing that environmental scientists who come to test these waters are amazed by how clean they are. They could not believe it and frankly, neither could I.

As he sipped his tea, he spoke of the happiness that I still knew so little about. He spoke of this happiness as if he knew no other emotion, as if there were no other emotions. And for him there was no reason not to be happy. He was born from these waters and here he will die, just as his father before him and his children after and if happiness were to be found in any other place other than Varanasi, he would not care to find it. For here was happiness. For a moment I wondered when it is, if it is, that I will ever find happiness. So little I knew of happiness, as reluctant to drink from its well as I was from the Ganges, that even if I were to find it, how would I know what it was?

Silence descended upon the city, but the fires never faded, they simply burned, a distant glow of embers, a searing reminder that life, in all its forms, goes on. In the subdued darkness, we parted ways, he into the heart of the city and I still on the surface. and I walked home, tracing the course of the river, tiptoeing among the stones and sleeping standing cows, careful not slip or stumble upon what lay waste in these alleys. Now, I could have been put off by this filth, but this refuse was no different from what I had done to my heart for so years and who was I to judge a country when I treated the country of my soul the very same way? Besides, here spirituality is something so intimate that it shares the same space as the air that fills my lungs and with each breath I began to understand that it will take lifetimes to understand the meaning of happiness, to understand the meaning of life and as I climbed up the steep steps of the ghat I began to quietly accept happiness for what it is: an ephemerality meant to last for a moment and no more.

Goa in the beginning of May is so very quiet except for the heat that screams in the sun and even in the shade. As the sun hid behind clouds, I walked along this stretch of sand: the only border between India and the Arabian Sea. The water was warm, the temperature warmer. The air was thick with salt and the only way to tell time was by the rising and the falling of the tides. In this way an eternity passes in a day and here I learned what it means to be still. Gone now were the tourists and the beaches were almost empty save for stray dogs, sacred cows, and every now and again a white and wild horse. Young men bare of torso shuffled their feet in the sand to make a cricket pitch. Then they bowled to one another laughing, playing with tennis balls and bats made from driftwood and fallen trees. In between pitches they tumbled into the ocean and returned, cool and covered in sand to play another round.

In Goa, I began to embrace the slowness of this journey in which schedules barely existed and days of the week no longer mattered. Hours became arbitrary. Days passed and I neither mourned their passage nor cared where they went.

In the white heat of the mornings I drank French pressed coffee at a table that faced the Arabian Sea. As if desperate to hold onto even more heat, I clasped the coffee cup in both hands and wrapped my fingers underneath the porcelain before each sip. What breeze there was slowed and stopped before the noonday sun. Hungry, always hungry, I ordered a breakfast that raised the bar for all other breakfasts to come: crepes with lime, sprinkled with cinnamon, and drizzled with

27

honey. The crepes were both thick and thin as if they had ideas of becoming pancakes and then thought better of it, the lime had just been plucked from nearby trees, the cinnamon was grated into tiny pebbles; small stones of spice, and the honey was so sweet that it fell like syrup onto the plate. Since arriving in these lands I have learned that the food of India is a journey in itself and it is in the eating of these meals, using my thumb as a fork, my fingers as a spoon, that I learned what it is like to fall in love again: slowly now for there is no rush. Each piece of naan bread, each leaf of mint, each bite of vegetable biryani, and every sip of lime soda was a tumble towards ecstasy and these combinations of ingredients forever changed the way a lemon, a tomato, and even a single grain of rice was seen. As I took one last bite I thought to myself that if food was not to be part of this journey, I might have never left for what better way is there to connect with the world than to share meals, to share thoughts, and to share prayers? And these meals, where there is spice on the lips and sweetness on the tongue, have become like prayers, and I offered my thanks to whichever gods might hear them.

For what remained of the week I spent the early and late hours of the day watching waves crash onto the shore. From dry land they were docile, cresting and undulating in steady rhythms, but swimming in the currents the water became what it is: a force of nature, a power intoxicating. Emerging from the ocean, I sat wet without a towel gathering handfuls of sand before letting them slip back into the sea, thinking only of this: how I wished on this journey to go from the rock that I try so very hard to be into a single grain of sand. The water rushed in, carrying away my wishes. Maybe they will one day come true.

At night I went by myself back to the sands and waited for the stars to appear in clusters and

28

constellations. Everywhere there was darkness. Everywhere there was light.

Although it was past midnight I could not sleep; awake with the awareness that I was on the wrong side of the sea, for it was the lands across this ocean that called my name. Soon enough there I would be, but for now, I was here. For now, I was in India. Eventually sleep did arrive, ridden on the backs of waves that roared and whispered only this:

"This is India, Madam. Nothing is impossible."

To Kate I returned for one last night and we shared one last meal. Here she was to stay and I to travel westward where this pilgrimage was to begin in earnest.

Entering India, I knew nothing. Leaving I knew nothing still and perhaps that was the way it was meant to stay; a mystery, one of the few left, and no more.

IF ANOTHER HEAVEN
EXISTS, I WILL NOT GO

On the second Monday of May my plane landed on a strip of land nestled between mountains and the Mediterranean as the sun made its slow descent into the sea. Entering the airport, I hid my passport in the folds of my arms fearful to reveal the blue of its cover and the emblem of an eagle on the front page. Ahead the line grew shorter. When finally, it was my turn I cautiously slipped my passport to the customs official, wanting only him to know that I was American and no one else, but he barely looked up as he carelessly leafed through its pages.

"Is this your first time to Lebanon?" he asked.

Yes, was my answer even though I already knew it was not to be my last.

"Welcome to Lebanon," he said, smiling and stamping my passport before returning it without so much as pomp or circumstance.

Outside taxis lined the curb. I hailed the first that was found, and we drove across the city. Free of the oppressive heat of India I rolled down the windows to welcome the air of the sea, full of salt and hope. The sun continued to move west, casting shadows across the city. Soon the day would end. As we weaved wildly through traffic, the taxi driver took long drags from his cigarette, the plumes of smoke rising toward the felted roof. He inhaled deeply and with each exhale the smoke whirled higher and then disappeared into the approaching dusk. Driving through the center of the city, we passed the Blue Mosque, its minarets rising from its corners, its dome mirroring the late spring sky. Beyond the mosque was Martyrs Square, a monument commemorating the men, women, and children who were executed in Lebanon during Ottoman Rule. This landmark also represents the line of demarcation during the Lebanese Civil War. For fifteen years it divided the city between Christian and Muslim, East and West, war and peace.

Once at the hostel, the last of the golden light glinted off the crosses that adorned the steeples of the Orthodox Armenian churches that rose like hope above the skyline. And then it was dark. The hostel was on the third floor and I walked slowly up the stairs in the quickening darkness. Once at the top, I was greeted by Maryam. She sat behind a desk that hid most of her body, but none of her spirit. She wore red- rimmed glasses, her hair falling about her face, so thick and curly that it forever remained untamed. Her eyes were wide and wise as if she both knew the world and was only seeing it for the first time. She smiled as I entered, opening her arms for an embrace that included not two but three kisses. This is the Middle Eastern way. The warmth of her greeting reminded me of all the conversations we had had before through email and now, face-to-face, we spoke as if old friends. In a matter of moments, she led me to the room that was to be my home for the next few weeks: a four-bed dorm that opened to views of surrounding apartments and the balcony below.

Hungry I set my bags down and then out to explore this new country, hoping to get lost in mezze and nowhere else. The streets were dimly lit and many of the shops in this more residential neighborhood of Beirut were already closed for the night. Around a darkened corner a small restaurant was found where I ordered my first meal in Lebanon: hummus, thereafter always hummus. It was drizzled with olive oil thick and warm, as if the flesh of the olives had just been separated from their stones. As in India, I ate slowly, wanting to remember the way the flat bread felt between my fingers and the taste of chickpeas on my tongue. In all the years of making hummus, nothing compared to this. I closed my eyes to take one last delicious bite and then returned to the hostel.

In the common area other travelers were gathered. No sooner did I come back then did I leave again, this time in the company of Shadi, a young Christian refugee from Syria who had only recently taken up residence in Beirut and Jeremy, a psychologist from Australia who came to Lebanon on holiday from his job as a trauma counselor in the Palestinian city of Ramallah. Both were hungry, for food, for conversation, for life; for sometimes what feeds the stomach and what feeds the soul is one in the same.

As the hour approached midnight, we walked the streets determined to find something that was still open. Soon we stumbled into a restaurant flooded with fluorescent lights that brightened and blurred the surrounding street, where we sat at a table with red plastic chairs. Shadi and Jeremy ate French fries and falafel. In between bites, they spoke in English and Arabic, alternating between the two as if putting together missing pieces of a puzzle one word at a time. Both in their twenties, Jeremy was tall and lean with a playful intelligence, which made it difficult to determine when to take him seriously and when to not. He spoke with conviction of the things he was passionate about: pretty girls, Aussie rules football, and politics. Shadi had a soft smile and eyes so deep that it was hard to tell, when looking into them, whether he was near or far away. They both spoke of lost countries: Jeremy of Palestina and Shadi of a home in Syria that he may never call home again. When all the fries were finished, we retraced our steps back to the hostel and said goodnight in the hallway. That first night I had the room all to myself; a luxury never to be taken for granted in the whirlwind world of backpacking where people come and go in the middle of the night without thoughts of silence or darkness, but tonight the room was quiet and soon I was asleep.

In Arabic, the word for this region is *Mashriq*, meaning the land where the sun rises. The name is derived from the verb sharaqa, which means, "to shine, illuminate, radiate." And when day broke, the sun rose, illuminating the space between buildings, casting shadows and spreading light.

Beirut is believed to be one of the oldest inhabited cities in the world, tracing its foundation back over five thousand years to the time of the Phoenicians. Since then it has been home to Greeks, Romans, Arabs, and Ottomans. For centuries, Beirut has served as the gateway to the East, an invitation to the west, and a crossroads between three continents.

It was my first time in the Middle East, and I walked with quiet trepidation through the empty streets.

35

All the shops were closed, none of the windows open, for Lebanon is no place for early risers. It awakens like a cat from a nap stretching and yawning away the night without care of rushing into the day. Then it starts slowly, with a cup of coffee, perhaps even two, before the day can truly begin.

Outside, the air was full of what only spring can promise: an unbounded continuation of life. Jacaranda trees bloomed full and the world was colored purple; even the sky. In Beirut, the smell of jasmine swept through the streets with such sweet suddenness that I had to stop and beg for this spring to stay forever, if only just to remember this heavenly gift.

The whole of that first day was spent meandering through the streets of Beirut, climbing up and down steep stairs colored with graffiti in Arabic, French, and English that called for truth and cried for freedom. By eventide, I found myself as far as the sea to watch the sun sink into the Mediterranean. Along the Corniche, a ledged road separating the city from the sea, women with heads covered and uncovered laughed and posed for selfies in the fading light. Fathers played soccer with their daughters and young boys fished, casting their lines into the cobalt waters, hoping to catch something in their lures. Among the rocks old men sat at small tables, playing cards as they smoked cigarettes; perhaps as they have done their whole lives and would continue to do so until the end.

When the sun touched the sea, the city erupted in a song ushered from the surrounding mosques. It was the adhan, the Muslim call to prayer. The first phrase was familiar, *Allahu Akbar*. What followed, the *shahad*a, less. It echoed from the minarets that lit green in the twilight and was carried like wind across the city. All around life went on but for me the world slowed except for the tears that rushed down my cheeks, flushed with fever for a god

36

I have never known. In India the adhan must have been missed but to miss it now in Beirut would have been impossible and I promised myself to listen for it always and never miss it again. The sky darkened, the sun set, but never had I felt so surrounded by light.

The next day was no different and more hours were spent walking back and forth the length and width of the city. Before the Lebanese Civil War began in 1975, Beirut was deemed "The Paris of the East," but fifteen years of war destroyed much of the city and what remained was still in the process of being rebuilt. At first it was difficult to believe that there had been a war, so vibrant were the streets of Beirut that it was almost easy to forget. Almost, until stumbling upon buildings riddled with bullets on the verge of collapse. There were no roofs, no windows, just broken doors that have not been entered, or exited, since. Stand in front of these houses and only war might be remembered and nothing else. I wondered, if studied long enough, might a geologist of war be able to ascertain what year of the war these walls were penetrated by shells. Was it the beginning, the middle, or the end? Was it the first bullet or was it the last? And yet, from the foundation of these houses, without walls, grew trees, their leaves green with spring, their limbs and crowns spreading like ceilings; enough cracks had been created for life to seep through.

For hours and hours, I continued to walk the streets of Beirut. One side rang with church bells and the other, muezzins. Even years after the Civil War, the city is still divided along religious lines, separating the past from the future, making it difficult to tell which is more uncertain. This same uncertainty is found in the sidewalks of Beirut, which vary in width from the very narrow to the very wide. Often, they change in a matter of steps, which made walking in Beirut both a challenge and an adventure. In the first week I took up an old favorite of mine whose legality is questionable back in the United States: jaywalking. It is, after all, the only way to maneuver the sidewalks that end just as suddenly as they begin.

The light of Beirut also shifts like the sidewalks, creating shadows where once there was sun and offering light where there is darkness. But the way is illuminated more than it is obscured and where I thought I might encounter hostility, I was met instead with smiles from soldiers, the curiosity of children, and the gift of a magnolia blossom from a stranger on the street. All of this ensured the impossibility of superficiality in Lebanon, for to enter this country is to step into the very heart and soul of this land, plunging into unimaginable depths and never wanting again to resurface. So warm was the welcome of Beirut, so fervent its embrace that somehow, finally, the past and future collapsed into the present rendering any notion of time unnecessary, which is why, in Beirut, it is important to be present, always present, because that is where the beauty lies.

Thereafter, every day was more of the same, except more: more warmth, more smiles, more food, and more generosity than ever imagined. It was more than enough to make you wonder how one side of the world could be so very different from the other and how one side could be so fearful of the other.

All of this kindness almost surprised me because days before my departure my aunt forwarded me a warning issued by the State Department advising citizens of the United States not to travel to Lebanon and yet here I was, weeks later, happy to have not listened to a woman who loved me the only way she knew how: in one piece.

Would that I could tell her that never had I felt so whole.

In the afternoons an eclectic group of internationals always gathered on the balcony of the hostel where they smoked cigarettes, drank Arak, and talked about all the reasons why they were in Beirut. Often, I found myself the lone American among Europeans trying to explain to a continent how it is that Donald Trump came to be elected President of the United States. It was a conversation that was to be had in every country that I traveled, but it never was easy to explain, let alone understand. As it was my father, the man who I spoke to about everything, and I had stopped speaking to one another in civil tones both before and after the election. That, to me, was more difficult to accept than America's propensity towards drama and grandeur. How could I be so very far from my father and not tell him of what it was like to travel to Lebanon forty years after he did? How could I not tell him of the best hummus in the world? Then again it was my hope that if I could better understand the ways in which a world so old worked, then maybe I could then understand the new. But all these afternoon discussions revealed only how easy it was for foreigners to come to the Middle East and offer what little they knew of peace.

As we spoke a woman lounged in the shadows of the sun, listening but staying silent. Her short sleeves and shorter shorts revealed her sun kissed arms and legs. In between drags of her hand-rolled cigarette, she spoke above the others:

"My name is Briana, I am American, and I have opinions," she quipped, her accent thick with sarcasm and antipodean charm. With a statement as bold and true as that, I had no choice but to respect her. So quick was this lesson, so abrupt its delivery, that I did not offer a retort to the contrary. How could I? She was right. Her name was Joanne. Australian, she had just spent the greater part of the year living and working in Jordan as a dive instructor. Her eyes were a bright blue, like the sea she so loved, and her crooked smile convinced me that somehow, she still had all her trouble making years in front of her rather than behind.

That night she introduced more of the beauty of the Levant to me: the food, the men, and Arabic words not yet known to my ears. We dined until midnight sharing small dishes that somehow seemed bigger: fatoush, tabbouleh, hummus, octopus, all of it accompanied by olive oil that made even my Italian cheeks blush. We ate with our hands or with bread so thin that it was almost transparent, tearing and folding it between our fingers before dipping it into the feast before us. I had to remind myself to eat with intention, for to eat quickly is to forget; to eat slowly, to delight. After all was finished, it would have been impossible to eat more, we walked back to the hostel with swollen bellies under a swollen moon.

Most nights, before sleep Shadi would come to my room, leaving the door open just enough to let the light in. In the remaining darkness he sat on the edge of the bed and together we talked of our days, our lives, our fears and our dreams. When Shadi spoke of his home there was lament in his voice for he knew that to leave Syria was to live, to stay meant almost certain death. Everyday Shadi was torn between his country and his life as if one could not possibly exist without the other. Shadi knew more English than I knew Arabic, but still we practiced learning the language of the other. If ever he grew frustrated, he would smile, tisk his tongue and say, *la la la*, no no no. But his frustration was not borne from

40

my failure to understand him, it was from his failure to understand the world.

From Shadi I learned all the things that are permissible in Lebanon. For all the times I said to him, "I can't do that!" he responded with two words that always convinced me otherwise: "You can!" Maybe here, like India, nothing was impossible.

For Shadi, everything was too much. He emphasized his vowels, elongated them into the night and when he spoke these two words, he said them in such a way that there was no other choice but to agree. From then on everything encountered in Lebanon was too much: Too much beauty. Too much history. Too much war.

Too much. Too much. Too much.

In the mornings *man'oushe*, a traditional Lebanese breakfast, was set out on the table downstairs and covered with a towel to stay warm. The surface of the bread is dusted in *zataar*, a blend spices: wild thyme, oregano, cumin, coriander and sumac; the inside is filled with cheese. Those who were awake cut small pieces from the bounty, careful to save some for those who still slept. They ate in silence, drinking their Nescafé in the quiet solitude of morning. After, they smoked their first cigarette of the day, smiling before bringing it to their lips, as if they had woken up just for this small satisfaction.

At the table I sat with Cyril, a young man from France, who was studying Arabic and Middle Eastern

41

politics, making plans to travel to Tripoli together because we were told by Maryam that it was not always best to go alone, for recently Tripoli had been the site of skirmishes resulting from tensions brought on with the war in Syria. Maryam also told us that Tripoli is where the best knefeh, her favorite dessert, can be found. It is made from semolina dough layered with ackawi cheese, then sprinkled with pistachios, and drizzled in rose water. On the way out the door we promised to bring her back some and even promised to come back in one piece.

After breakfast we took a van north, hailing a gypsy cab on the side of the highway with well-worn seats and air full of acrid smoke; these gypsy cabs are how those without cars get from place to place. Left wanting in the years after the war, Lebanon is not celebrated for its infrastructure, rather it laments in its lack thereof. The road was marked with checkpoints, small concrete stands in the middle of the highway where soldiers dressed in gray fatigues and red berets keep guard. At each the young uniformed men waved us through, smiling as we continued north.

To Tripoli we went to see the largest crusader castle in all of Lebanon: The Citadel of Raymond de Saint-Gilles. After the Crusaders captured Jerusalem from the Fatimid Caliphate in 1099, they set their eyes on the Lebanese coast, first capturing Tripoli, then Beirut and Sidon, and finally Tyre in 1124. Their presence is still seen in the castles, ramparts, and Christian churches along the coast. We arrived mid-morning just as the streets began to fill with merchants and merchandise. We walked towards the castle weaving through the streets of the souk covered in black tarp above and dirt below. Like Beirut, bullets are buried in the walls of Tripoli, remnants of sectarian violence that surged during the uprising in Syria.

Although the citadel was built almost a thousand years before much was still intact and the rest of the morning was spent exploring every corner of the castle before climbing to the top where we were greeted with a view of mountains to the east, the sea to the west, and above us only sky. Coming down from the castle we drank fresh squeezed juice and ate falafel, still hot, the outside crisp, the inside crumbling and returned to Beirut full of food and history.

The next day we were joined by Theo, a man from the Netherlands and Joanne, the Australian. The four of us traveled to the ancient city of Baalbek, formerly known as Heliopolis, the city of the sun. Just after breakfast we clamored into a van and made our way back north. Baalbek is situated just fifty-three miles northeast of Beirut and forty-seven miles from Damascus. It is home to some of the best-preserved Roman ruins in all of Lebanon and perhaps even the world.

Let out in the center of the city, we walked the kilometer or so to the temples of Baalbek, passing fields of poppies and even one of the largest monolithic stones ever excavated. Along the road we also passed a small apartment complex. It might have gone unnoticed: an unimposing wall of concrete with few windows to speak of, but inside the courtyard hung small flags and banners that reminded us where we were: Hezbollah territory. Instinctively, Joanne raised her camera and pointed it in the direction of an image of a Hezbollah leader that was strung between the buildings, but the men who sat outside on their plastic chairs, smoking their cigarettes and drinking their coffee, tsked their tongues, shook their heads, and told her 'no photo.' There was no need to tell her twice and she lowered her camera as quickly as it was raised. Today might have been one for adventures, but it was not a day for unnecessary risks.

Once at the gates of Baalbek, I did not wait to enter. Art historian that I am, I live for moments just like this. Inside, columns loomed so large that they hid the sun that they were meant to revere. I walked up to each column, tracing my fingers along the ribs of their bodies, feeling its polished pores and the grittiness of its disintegration, imagining the mountains they once were. Somewhere between all that still stands and that which has fallen I remembered a paper I had written in graduate school about the Sol Invictus, the Unconquerable Sun, and its presence among Roman Temples in both the far reaches of its empire and in Rome itself. Did my heart, all those years ago, lead me to where I found myself that day? Maybe it did. Maybe it always knew I would seek the sun. We stayed form much of the afternoon, climbing among the ruins, visiting Venus in her temple, and celebrating Bacchus. Before leaving I turned around for one last glimpse of Baalbek, whispering in Latin as the Romans did, *Veni Vedi Vici* and then like the past it was gone.

On Thursday there were only three of us: Cyril, Theo, and me. Rather than waiting for a bus that did not depart until it was full, we hired a cab to take us to Tyre, a city south of Beirut. We shared this cab with a young Palestinian man who had come from Dubai to visit his family in Beirut. Much of his family had been here since 1948, they had been among the first to flee Palestine during the Nakba, or the "catastrophe." A tragic disaster where 700,000 Palestinians were forced from their homeland, never to return. In his hands he held a piece of paper that measured eight inches by eleven. It was covered in plastic and so much larger than the passport I had carefully tucked away in the small pocket of my bag. Naïvely I asked what it was. With anguish he responded that it was what identified him as a Palestinian, as a man belonging to no land and having no country to call his own. His voice carried with it a grief of unfathomable depths. He spoke with the soft hesitation of a man for whom the word home had not a meaning for he had never been to Palestine and might never go, but like the paper in his hands he held it tightly, unable to let it go. He did not travel as far as us that day, but we stayed silent after he left; what words can be spoken about the unspeakable?

For thousands of years the city of Tyre flourished as a port for Phoenicians, Romans and even Ottomans. But now, so far removed from the glory of its past and so close to Lebanon's neighbors to the south, the ruins are subject to looting and pollution.

The road to the ruins is wide and covered in stones and weeds that leads to the oblong track of the hippodrome, still visible, and the spina, though fractured, still stands in its center. Around and around the circus Maximus we walked imagining the roar of the crowds and the clash of the chariots. Somewhere in the middle I stood where Alexander the Great might once have stood and imagined him there looking east and then looking west; wanting nothing more than to conquer the world.

Walking further through the ruins, towards the columned causeway the sea shifted from cobalt to indigo, as did the clouds. I, too, looked left, then right at all that remains: broken columns and shattered mosaics, wildflowers and a wide and wild sea. Among the ruins I thought of how many civilizations have been destroyed, not by the hands of time, but at the hands of men and in this destruction, history no longer has an opportunity to repeat itself. It simply must begin again.

With each passing week I grew braver, realizing there is less to fear in Lebanon than previously believed. Because of this I boarded a bus by myself to Byblos, sharing a seat with a woman who was returning from Beirut to visit her family. We sat shoulder-to-shoulder, knee-to-knee and laughed with one another over every bump in the road, of which there were many. The bus sped down the highway and only when a bell was rung did the driver slam on his brakes catapulting whoever it was who was standing to the front of the bus. As we drove further north, she invited me to her party, but without a SIM card and without Wi-Fi there would have been no way to reach her and I was sad to tell her no. The bus stopped and before she got off, we hugged one. As the bus pulled away I thought that even though these kinds of invitations happen so often in Lebanon I know better than to expect this kindness, I only accept it, hoping beyond hope that one day I am able to return this kindness to whomever, wherever in the world.

Byblos, also known as Jbeil, traces its roots back over ten thousand years and like many cities in the Levant it is said to be one of the oldest continuously inhabited cities in the world. Here lived Phoenicians, Persians, Romans, and even those from more distant shores. In Byblos there is another castle that was used by Crusaders in the twelfth century. Over the course of the Crusades the castle changed hands between the Christian west and the Islamic east. A millennia later it still stands.

Inside, surrounded by thick stone walls I weaved my way up the stairs smoothed by centuries, to the very top, which opened to a panorama of Byblos. Although it was not yet summer the heat rose bringing with its warmth and solace.

Hours were spent exploring every corner of this castle, running my hands along the roughness of the rocks and stumbling upon the stones. Beyond the well-worn path there is a Persian Gate with the head of a lion still visible after thousands of years. Its eyes open, its mouth closed as if sworn to silence but not to sight. I, too, was silent, reveling in a day like no other. Here was happiness that I had been seeking, if only I was ready to accept it.

The wind came and brought with it the salt of the sea, the warmth of the sun, and the scent of jasmine and orange blossoms. Behind the castle, the hills rose as if in want of a better view. The sea was every color blue: turquoise, azure and sapphire. It crashed into the shore as if finally learning what it was like to return home. For the whole of the afternoon, the wind never ceased, it blew warm and soft and among the wildflowers. I walked among them, as they swayed from side to side, bending and bowing to the wind, thinking how the wind is many things, but never a liar. A single gust alone can betray the years that have passed by sweeping them away in a matter of moments, carrying us from our present into our past without care of whether that was where we wanted to go. Before leaving the castle, facing the wind, I whispered to it:

"Come for me. Come for me often and take me back to this day, the best of my life."

Outside the gates of the citadel there is a mosque, its single minaret piercing the clouds and even the sky. Upon leaving the castle the call to prayer began, the first words echoing from the mountains to the sea. I closed my eyes and opened my heart to make space for this moment, allowing this song to fill all that might still be empty inside of me and for the briefest of moments I was full. Slowly, I walked away from the Citadel reminding myself that I know nothing of Islam save for

47

this. It is only now that I am learning the ninety-nine names of god.

After, I wandered the cobbled streets intoxicated by the spring of Lebanon. Before me, the city stretched like a canvas painted in the purples that made Phoenicia famous. Early in the evening I found myself alone at a table under a trellis of jasmine and jacaranda where a feast of mezze was ordered: fatoush, libneh, and maghmour; my daily sustenance in Lebanon from which I never tired, I only hungered for more. Bread, still warm and rising from the oven, was brought to the table. Tearing from its edges, steam escaped and swirled around jars of mint, radishes and olives before disappearing like smoke in the air. I reached for an olive, sliding it from my fingers to my lips and then the world, always so determined to go on, stopped. From the flesh came the taste of lemons, of liquid, of life. Never had I tasted something so perfect, not until Lebanon, not until this. Again, I closed my eyes and returned to the place where revelry and reverence are one and the same. Pulling the pit from my mouth, not yet ready to part with its flesh, I learned in that moment only this:

Let the small surprise you. Let it fill you up. Let it make you whole.

Surrendering myself to what remained of the day I stood on an ancient sea wall waiting for the sun to set, which was still warm against my skin. Lightning streaked across the sky. I listened for thunder and waited for rain. But the rain would not come. Not here. Not yet. And still the wind. Eventually the sun sank into the far away west, flashing green on the horizon, a last light before darkness, and then it was night.

In the morning, before returning to Beirut, I went to the Armenian Genocide Orphan's Museum to learn of an often-unspoken history. Even after 10 a.m., I was the first and only person to arrive at its gates. My dearest friend, my RHB, is of Armenian descent. Over the course of our friendship she has shared stories of all of the nights she was kept awake by the cries of her great grandmother who escaped the violence in Armenia in 1915, a violence that began the year before and did not end until 1923. She arrived in America shortly after, but never could she forget the war or the country she left behind.

The museum is small like a chapel, with brick walls accented by soft light as songs sung in Armenian echo throughout the chambers. The lights grew brighter and more of the museum came into view, but I hesitated to take any more steps. To move would be to move into a violent past in which mothers and fathers disappeared, villages were destroyed, children were displaced and deported, and one and a half million Armenians were killed. To move would be to step into a history that has been repeated time and time again in so many more places to so many more people despite our loudest protestations of never again.

The walls were covered in sepia toned photographs, portraits of Armenian children who lived and died during the eight years of genocide, their clothes ragged, their feet covered in dust and dirt. In silence I stayed, memorizing their eyes, their hands, their faces, wondering how many of these children still live, how many of them have returned to Armenia and how many could never go back.

Outside again, beyond the walls of the museum, clouds gathered again in the mountains, but they held no rain. In the garden lemon trees opened their leaves to the sun and wildflowers bloomed in the pinks and purples and reds of May. And yet, despite these signs of the persistence of life, I was reminded just how often in the spring, when the world so often gives birth, these genocides begin. Ever so solemnly I returned to Beirut wondering all the while if this violence will ever end?

Back in Beirut, the hostel was loud and crowded, but outside it was quiet save for the squealing of tires and the beeping of horns as cars jockeyed for the front lines of crosstown traffic. Restless, I walked across the city from Mar Mikhael to Raouche, Beirut's westernmost point. As the sun lowered itself to the horizon church bells clanged and the muezzin released its call to prayer. I stopped, offering prayers of my own to the coming darkness. The song faded and then awakened the soul of the city. Bars and restaurants, closed in the light of day, opened their doors, voices became louder, and cooler temperatures spread from the shadows. In every cafe and restaurant men and women smoked shisha, holding the pipe near their lips as they carelessly thumbed their cups of coffee. In passing they smiled, and I regretted that my Arabic, my French, and sometimes even my English were not enough to sustain a conversation. Still they welcomed me to their country. This constant reoccurrence reminded me of the opening scene in Pretty Woman when a man walks down a boulevard in Los Angeles saying to everyone he passes, "Welcome to Hollywood," so that when I was welcomed to Lebanon I wanted so badly to respond: "What's your dream?" But this, this was my dream. A dream made even more real because of the beauty I was now surrounded by; more beautiful than anything I had known before.

It did not escape notice that the people of Lebanon are as beautiful as their country, especially the men since they were all my type: tanned skin, dark eyes, dark hair, dark beards, reckless smiles and a confidence derived from speaking three languages and living on the edge of two worlds of which their beauty was just a reflection. But for this I will not hunger; this pilgrimage was not about this. In all my relationships in the past I had fallen too fast and too hard and it took me far too long to recover from the bumps and bruises of the way down. And now neither my heart nor my body was ready to invite a new love into these empty spaces. How could I possibly love another when the door of my heart was only ajar and not fully opened?

And so, as the evening unfolded, I sat alone at a table with my hummus. If there were a better date in all of Lebanon, I would not go on it, not for all the hummus in the world. Across the way a man spoke first in Arabic, then in French, and finally in English, of the truth of the human experience. Manners be damned I eavesdropped upon his words, needing to learn more of what he knew of truth and if it was different than my own. With him was a woman who spoke as much with her hands as she did her mouth. In gesticulations both wild and tame, she agreed with him before adding truths of her own. She smiled as if happiness was an old friend with whom she shared a secret that she will always keep. Before long I joined in their conversation. Her name was Mona and there was but four years between us. We spoke as if we had known one another always and were simply catching up on the years that had been missed. At the end of our meals we exchanged phone numbers and promised to call one another soon.

That Sunday, Mona invited me to spend the day with her family in the mountains. Before noon she picked me up at the end of Mar Mikhael and barely was the door

51

shut before she began to shout, curse, and beep her horn at all the other drivers for driving as they do in Lebanon: lawlessly. Had I been behind the wheel I would have done the very same thing. If there were any doubts about this new friendship they disappeared before we passed the limits of the city.

As we moved beyond Beirut, she told the stories of her life, her country, her loves, and the wars that she has lived through. She laughed nervously as she spoke about the years of the Civil War, which consumed her childhood and much of her adolescence. Driving further into the hills she recalled how upset she used to get with her mother for not taking her skiing during the Lebanese Civil War. She did not understand then that those mountains and her beliefs stood in opposition of one another. When she spoke of the early years in the underground bomb shelters that many Muslims took refuge in, it was almost in disbelief that there was a war above. She even hinted at rumors that Yasser Arafat used to hide alongside her family, smiling slyly as she whispered that he would often do so dressed as a woman. As they grew older and braver, she and her friends would go to parties at the places where bombs were dropped only hours before.

Maybe she believed bombs to be like lightning, rarely striking the same place twice.

She spoke of war as a joyful time full of laughter and an ineffable peace. It was not until later, much later that she began to realize what she had lived through: fifteen years of a war that she had been unlucky enough to have been born into and lucky enough to survive.

In the mountains her family keeps a house full of memories. This is where they come to celebrate birthdays, Sundays, Sabbath, and summer. This is also

52

the home that became a fortress during the Israeli invasion of 2006. As she spoke about that summer, she gripped the steering wheel tightly, in both of her hands, not wanting to remember, unable to forget. Although Mona had spoken about the years during the war, nothing compared to that July when fire rained down from the sky for thirty-four days, an assault that did not end until the United Nations called for a ceasefire between the two nations.

The house stands on top of a hill. It is the last on the left. Rose bushes lined the driveway, not yet in bloom; their red petals still clung tightly to their buds as if they were waiting for summer and not spring. Like the streets of Beirut, sensuous stalks of jasmine laced the wooden arbor and I could not, would not imagine Lebanon smelling any other way.

Mona's mother met us at the door and for a moment I forgot that I was in Lebanon and not New York. So warm was her embrace that for a moment I had forgotten that this was not my family. She easily could have been my aunt and Mona my cousin. The backyard overlooked the white mountains for which Lebanon receives its name. They spread east, separating Lebanon from Syria. In the shade of cedars sat her brother and sisters, their husbands and wives. On the edge of the hill there was an above ground pool where children splashed and played and invited me to join them; I did not wait to be asked twice for Sunday's are meant for just for this.

Under a rising moon we sat at a table surrounded by trees as tall as mountains. This table was no different than that of my mother's and like that of my mother's there was not an empty space to be found, not a seat that was not full. Everywhere were bowls of hummus, plates of fried fish, and salads of grains and greens. Everything was passed from hand to hand with a smile or a gentle nudge of the shoulder. When their

53

children tried to sneak past them, none of them got away without a hug and a kiss and a whisper of I love you. It reminded me of Christmas. It reminded me of home.

After the plates were emptied and our stomachs were full, I sat next to Mona's brother watching what remained of the sun escape from the day. At first, he did not speak, a quiet intensity in his silence, but then he casually stated:

"Mona tells me you are a writer."

I nodded, still learning to differentiate between when words are necessary and when they are not. One by one the stars appeared. The moon rose high, whiter than the mountains beyond, bathing the faces of his family in its light. He looked at them, remembering what peace there is to be found in the darkness, and then he turned to me, looked me in the eyes and said:

"You tell of this. You write of this."

Saying nothing more, he held his gaze on his family. Through his silence, he was asking for me to write of the heart of Lebanon; its beauty, its people, its kindness and its generosity. He was asking me to reveal the Lebanon that had been revealed to me; the Lebanon that is not often seen by the world outside.

When the world again fell silent, I looked at him and promised that I would tell of everything. I will write every word. For the purpose of this pilgrimage was to search, to seek, to find, to share; to do as Faulkner said and to write of the heart and not the glands. Night came and Mona and I returned to Beirut under a veil of clouds and stars.

To Lebanon I went to better understand war. For fifteen years, from 1975 to 1990, civil war had ravaged Lebanon; a war whose impact can still be felt and seen to this day. It was not only this war, but the wars of this often-misunderstood region that I wanted to understand; how they start, and how, if, or when they will end.

From Lebanon, Syria was only a nation away. Until 1918, after the fall of the Ottoman Empire, Lebanon was part of Greater Syria when England divided the world, forever altering the borders of the Levant and the ways in which the world was occupied. By 2017 the war in Syria had been raging for seven years with still no end in sight. It has been estimated that five hundred thousand Syrians have been killed since the conflict began and that over eleven million Syrians have fled their country to their surrounding neighbors of Turkey, Lebanon, Jordan, Egypt and Iraq, making a region not known for its stability even more unstable.

Until the war began in Syria, most of the refugees who had arrived in Lebanon have been from Palestine, expelled as they were from their homes and their land almost seventy years before when the state of Israel was created and the land of Palestine was slowly destroyed. But now, almost a decade into a conflict that shows no signs of stopping, almost one million Syrians have flooded across the Lebanese border, crowding an already crowded country. But with war seething throughout their land, where else were they to go?

What remained of May was spent volunteering at a school in Shatila for Syrian children. Since 1949 Shatila has been the home of Palestinian refugees expelled from their homeland during the Nakba. It measures one square kilometer and until war erupted in Syria it housed almost 10,000 Palestinian refugees. Since the Syrian War began, that number has swelled to an estimated 22,000 refugees; so many people, too many people, for so small a space.

In the mornings, just before nine, Eleanor, a journalist turned English teacher from Belgium, and I walked from the hostel to the highway to flag down a van as it passed. After the sliding door slammed shut, we weaved in and out of traffic as we moved from one side of the city to another, stopping just outside of the gates of Shatila. Once out of the van we added layers to our clothing, rolled down the legs of our pants, and covered our shoulders and arms. And then we entered Shatila.

On those first days I felt like an intruder trespassing somewhere I had no place to be. Who was I to come and go when others would give, have given, their lives for this freedom? Although it had not rained, water flooded the streets and dirt collected in the middle of the road; the sewer system was not designed to accommodate so many occupants within these crowded confines. Ever aware, Eleanor said this happened often, too often really, and we walked to the edges of the puddle, careful where we stepped.

Above us, electrical wires, tangled and suspended, were stung across the narrow streets; a canopy of electricity, a cover of darkness meant to provide light. In every alleyway hung posters of the resistance, Palestinian flags, and photographs of Yasser Arafat. This is how we knew how to find the otherwise unmarked entrance. The school in which we taught shares the building with Médecins Sans Frontiers. As we climbed the crowded stairs to the second floor, we passed young mothers who waited with their children sleeping in their arms. In the flickering light, I did not know whether to smile or to move in silence, knowing that to play either the spectator or the specter make me complicit in what I was now witnessing: the long term effects of gross violations of human rights.

56

Upstairs, the school was no more than four rooms filled with plastic tables and chairs. The children, the living casualties of war, were all under the age of eleven with the youngest having just turned five years old. Normally I am against voluntourism, knowing from experience that it does more harm than good, but so torn had I become between doing nothing and doing something that I chose this. I chose hope.

The first week went slowly but as days passed, we began to recognize the people who lived and worked in Shatila. A smile was offered here, a nod of the head there. These have always been my favorite ways to say hello. In the break between morning and afternoon classes we took coffee with Mahmoud, a Palestinian whose family has now been here for a generation. Between us we did not share enough words in the same language, but still we sat, he behind the counter and us in front to drink small strong cups of coffee. To pass the time, he offered us cigarettes, rolling them in his fingers, twisting one end and lighting the other. On the screen of his phone there was a photograph of his future bride. She is as beautiful as he is with eyes just as green and a smile that speaks of hidden joys that neither time nor distance nor displacement can strip from her. When the time came for us to return to school, we paid for our coffees and said our 'til tomorrows.

After class, we walked down streets crowded with taxis, cars and bicycles. On one side of the street there were carts full of oranges and watermelons, cauliflower and tomatoes. On the other there was a butcher's shop. Inside, there were no customers and the room was empty save for meat that hung from hooks along the wall. The butcher stood in the center, his apron smeared with blood, his body a silhouette. In his hands he held a clarinet, caressing the bell and the barrel gently with his fingers. Alone with his instrument, he closed his eyes and brought the reed to his already pursed lips. Taking a deep breath, he sighed into the instrument, his exhalations transforming into a melody that neither Eleanor nor I had ever heard and perhaps will never again but still we listened as his fingers moved over the keys and his body swayed, slowly, as if tired of motion yet longing to move freely. We walked on unwilling to intrude on this small semblance of peace.

A bakery stood on the corner. From the open door you could smell all the sweetness of the Middle East: honey and dates, cinnamon and pistachios. The counters and shelves were full of pastries, the pans wide and brimming with baklava, kataifi, and barazek. The baker, a middle-aged man from Syria, beckoned us in from the street and offered us a taste of everything that he had baked. He would not take no for an answer, persisting, as if wanting us to create memories of Syria just by taking small sweet parts of it with us. Wanting the very same thing, we said yes. Besides, when offered this sort of kindness, no is never the answer.

As we walked towards the gates of Shatila we passed a man who sat on a stoop; his years no more than mine. On the tips of his fingers he spun a fidget spinner. It was green and red, black and white like the colors of a country he has never known: Palestine. He never let it slow, never let it stop, not even when his daughter, perhaps three, maybe four years old, came and went from underneath his legs laughing and dancing between the shadows and the sun. His long hair was pulled back in a ponytail and he wore a baseball cap of some faraway team. Around his neck he wore a golden chain with a pendant in the shape of Palestine so close to his heart it was as if it was his heart itself; how heavy it must have hung. We sat with him on these small stairs as he told of his life Shatila. He works when there is work and studies in his free time. Aloud, he wondered why it is that he is even learning to speak English. It is of no use to him in this refugee camp except for conversations such as this. He closed his eyes and held his breath searching for words to explain the inexplicable. When he opened them again he watched as his daughter ran down the street to play with her friends, telling us of his fear that she may never know what it is like to grow up in any other place but a refugee camp; she may never, not ever, know peace. His eyes filled with tears as he said this, but he wiped them away before they fell. I wish I could have caught them, held him, lied to him and told him that everything was going to be ok, but we left him on the stoop and made our way to the gates of Shatila. Stealing a glance over my shoulder, I saw him still sitting on the edge of the step, staring at his fidget spinner, spinning it higher and higher until all the colors melted into one. When it finally fell, he did not pick it up, he only stared into a distance just out of reach.

We left, taking another bus across the city. As we merged into traffic the door to the van slid open, it had never really closed, and for what remained of the ride I too stared into the empty space, wondering what a difference there is between leaving and being left behind.

When the sky darkened and clouds came to cover the sun, I went back to the restaurant that Joanne and I first went, this time alone. It was still early in the evening. American, I still like to dine before ten, a habit I have yet to outgrow. Besides, at all times of day I am overcome with an insatiable hunger for communion:

with food, with nature, with humanity and tonight was no different.

A man from Syria worked at this restaurant. Like many men his age, rather than being forced to fight in a war he would not and could not believe in, he came to Lebanon so that he may still work to feed his family- and to survive. Knowing that my ears and my heart were his, he sat on his haunches and told stories of Syria, the beauty of his country, its food, and its people. He told me all of this as if returning to Syria in a dream instead of the nightmare it has become.

At the end of this meal small dishes filled with molasses and tahina were brought to the table. Swirling the two of them together I asked the one question that I already knew in my heart to be true:

"Tell me, is it true that Syria has the best baklava?" He smiled as if remembering a sweetness that can never be lost.

"Come back in two days, I will have something for you then."

Two days passed and I returned to the restaurant. He waved and smiled as I moved down the street, escaping inside for only a moment and then returning with two boxes, one brown, one blue, in his hands. He smiled again and I trembled as he offered this gift. It was baklava. From Syria. Never in the whole of my life have I received a greater gift. I wanted to say thank you, *shukran*, anything that might express gratitude for a gift that had shaken me to my very soul, but for this there were no words. Instead, there on the street, I began to cry. He did too. Unable to offer anything in return, I offered him my arms, wanting to hold onto his kindness forever. There we stayed, holding one another tight, each of us afraid to let the other go, as if there on that street we had found the meaning of humanity, as if we had found the meaning of life.

60

Returning to the hostel that night, I shared of his gift with everyone who was there. Taking small bites of baklava, I imagined that this was the way that Damascus tasted before the war and I wondered if, after the war, it would still taste this sweet.

In Saida, a city south of Beirut, there is another crusaders castle that stands in ruins by the sea. There, a causeway made from stones smoothed by the centuries and the tides leads out to the stronghold said once to be the site of a temple dedicated to the Phoenician god, Melqart, a deity of life, death and rebirth, but now little of the fortifications remain.

After exploring the ruins, I met a young brother and sister out on their afternoon walk. They were off to no place, and so we walked side by side by the sea. They, like many in Lebanon, were refugees escaping from the never-ending war in Syria. As we walked, I gazed west across the water, but their thoughts, like their hearts, flowed east, toward everything they have ever known.

How can anyone move forward when all they want to do is go back?

We continued together as far as the limits of the city, but they were only allowed to remain within the confines of Saida because of regulations that have been placed upon them as refugees. At the edge of the city they had to turn back lest they be stopped by the police for breaking a law that would never need to be abided by had there been no war. But there is a war, a war that rips families, homes, and countries apart. When they could go no further, we parted ways and I walked north to spend the afternoon sneaking into Phoenician ruins. There I wandered among half buried and broken columns and stone reliefs of god and mortals. Scrambling past a sign that read both in Arabic and English: Danger. Keep Out, I stepped back onto the road reeling at the thought of how unfair it is that some of us trespass and some of us are trespassed against.

In my last days in Lebanon I returned to Byblos to wander once more through the streets that had given me joy and granted me peace. The sun sank low to the horizon and it almost broke my heart to know that nothing could be done to stop this May from ending. When the night was veiled in darkness, I walked into a shop that sits along the sea. The owner, a portly man with more hair on his face than the top of his head, offered a special price for the trinkets that he sold. Wanting to relieve myself of burdens rather than add to them I accepted his offer of whiskey and cigarettes instead. Between drags and sips we spoke about politics and politicians, agreeing that the world would be better without than with.

A young man emerged from the back, his gaze steady, his gate confident. His hair was dark, his skin, olive, and his eyes spoke not only of this lifetime, but all the lifetimes he has lived before. In his arms he carried a violin; one of the few possessions he had brought with him when he fled from Syria. Without saying a word, he brought the violin to his shoulder, resting his chin on its edge. Sighing deeply, he lowered the bow, pulling it and pushing it across the strings, slowly at first and then in a crescendo, telling stories without words; lamentations of what has been lost and may never again be found. It was a song that echoed across eternities.

When the last of the notes disappeared into the night, he lowered his violin, but kept his eyes closed. As did I. How desperately I wanted this moment never to end. Silent we stayed for yet another eternity. He lost is his thoughts, I in mine. The day ended; the song still echoing across the sea.

On the Saturday before my departure I returned to Mona's house to celebrate Ramadan with her family, which had only begun the week before. With me I brought the box of baklava to thank them for their love and generosity. After all, what good is kindness if it is not shared? Just as the sun offered itself to night, we broke our fast, sharing one final meal together. As I looked around the table at four generations of family I realized how easy it might have been to come to Beirut in search only of war, for here it is easily found, but to seek out only death, violence, and destruction is to forget the adamancy of life to go on. And in Beirut, where life continues most fiercely is at the table where every meal is a celebration, a commodity greater than money, for this is what sustains life, and this last meal was no exception, full of the same food as the first and then some more.

While at this table I made the slow discovery that the food and the people of Lebanon are no different from one another. Both like to tell stories, both hold warmth that I hope to always encounter, but never compare, for the rest of this journey, and both have left me with a fullness that I hope will sustain me for all of the months to come.

I was sad to leave Mona but thanked her and her family for welcoming me to their table and allowing me to share in this feast called life.

Walking back to the hostel, I thanked Lebanon for everything it had given me this past month. I thanked Lebanon for the strength of its coffee, which awakened in me passions that I have allowed to sleep for far too long. For the simplicity of its mezze, which gave me pause to contemplate the richness of life, sometimes in the form of a mint leaf and sometimes in the form of a single olive. And, for its deserts, which humbled me to the sweetness of its generosity.

Crossing the city one last time I realized that until Lebanon I had no idea what beauty was, I had no idea what kindness was and it was in Lebanon that I learned something of beauty, something of kindness, and something of grace.

In Lebanon, I felt as if I had returned to the arms of a lover who, after having experienced the rebirth of spring, the gentleness of summer, the lightness of autumn, and his own winter darkness, had welcomed me back into his arms to share all that was learned from these seasons. In his arms he also held the bounty of this break, of which he was more than willing to share. "Try this," he said. "Taste this. See this. Smell this. Feel this." And so, I tried everything, I tasted everything, I saw, I smelled, I felt everything and from this affection I will no longer hide, I will not even try to escape from its never-ending embrace. And for this, Lebanon has either ruined me for all other places or made them all the more bittersweet.

You can keep your Paris. I will take my Beirut.

In the Land of
Pink Wind

With June returned the heat; a heat with no pause, no breath, no life. I arrived in Jordan just days after Ramadan began. Now with a visa issued I stood with more confidence in the customs line. When it was my turn, I handed the official the proper documents in the hope that I would be ushered through as quickly as in Lebanon, but he deliberated a little longer until finally he gruffly said, "Welcome to Jordan." Always grateful, I thanked him and went outside to find a cab that would take me to Amman.

Once on the highway it was difficult to tell where the earth ended, and the sky began for the horizon constantly undulated in waves of desert heat. The stark landscape expanded ever forward in never ending hills and valleys of sand, stone, and dust, hiding the past, erasing the present and making the future what it already is: a mirage.

In the distance the city rose white from the pink earth. Closer to the capital the once open roads grew more congested. Like Beirut, lanes in Amman were arbitrary and the green and red of stoplights were open for interpretation. With some difficulty we found the hotel that I was to stay under an overpass of King Ali Bin Al Husein Street. Its photographs did it more justice than it deserved, but the manager was kind and although born in Jordan, had spent his formative years in the hills of North Carolina racing cars and chasing women and for the first time on my trip I was happy to hear an American accent, even if it was drawn from below the Mason-Dixon line.

Inside, the hotel had all the makings of a B-rated horror film. The fan clicked and shook as it turned, the blades blurring the fluorescent light that fluttered on and off in the dim shadows of the room. Windows, sealed shut by time and paint, looked out onto a courtyard where concrete slabs and cinder blocks covered the ground and piles of dirt filled the corners. The hotel seemed to have been under construction since the Romans last occupied Amman, but in this desert, there was running water, sheets, however clean, and for the first time in weeks I was alone in a room that I had to share with no other. In the middle of the day, at the beginning of Ramadan, nothing was open and would stay that way until the sun fell from the sky and the moon rose to take its place. Without anywhere to be I laid down for an afternoon nap. The city could wait.

After a fretful sleep, I walked under a fierce and relentless sun into the center of the city. Now I have always been the hungry sort: hungry for love, hungry for laughter, hungry for life, but mostly hungry for food so that when I entered the market my stomach leapt almost as high as my heart just at the sight of it all. Here, under canopies that covered what roofs did not, men called to one another over the crowds, their baritone voices singing the songs of dates, apricots, and pomegranates and it was difficult to tell what was sweeter: the sound of their song or the fruits of their labor. Through the narrow paths, laden with bushels of spices, loose teas, and nuts, women walked in burkas and hijabs gathering what was needed for Iftar. In their hands they carried breads sprinkled with anise and sesame, the scents of which wafted through the corridor crowding the already crowded space with aromas of licorice and musk. What Herculean strength it must have taken not to break off one small morsel, but none passed their lips.

On small tables that stretched from one end of the market to the other there were figs as green as the first leaves of spring, their flesh plump and inviting, a kilo for fourteen Jordanian dinars, one for a wink and a smile. There were grapes too and melons of every color flesh. I stood in the middle of the alley wanting nothing more than to listen to this symphony of sights, smells, and sounds. Had it not been for the Arabic being spoken I might have felt as if this were Arthur Avenue in New York; if Beirut is the Paris of the East, then surely Amman must be the Bronx.

Leaving the market, I climbed to the top of the citadel as my lungs protested all they have been asked to breathe for the past six weeks: cigarettes, exhaust fumes, smog, and pollution. There the Temple of Hercules lay in ruins and the face of a gorgon, eyes wide, mouth open, peeked out from under weeds and other fallen things. The few columns that still stood, just as bare at the bottom as they were at the top, spoke of mortality, impermanence, and the futility of man. A flock of birds ascended and descended in the sky, changing directions and colors in midflight and the seven sandstone hills of Amman blushed in the paling light.

When the sky deepened to red the minarets of Amman lit green and firecrackers exploded across the city. Then came the call to prayer. I paused, closing my eyes to all but this. It echoed across Amman, escaping from the hills only to return to them again. How it echoed in the deepest depths of my soul. Unlike my Catholic upbringing, I was not asked to practice Islam. I was never made to go to a mosque as I was to church and never have I received a catechism to enter the Muslim faith. And yet somehow these prayers have become my baptism, a flood in the desert. The city stirred. Restless, it knew that the sun had set and Iftar could begin.

On a quiet street, away from the center of the city, there was a shop. On either side of the entrance herbs and spices spilled from burlap sacks and candies wrapped in cellophane glittered in the fading light. In the open doorway there was a young man, no more than a teenager who might soon be twenty. We smiled to one another as I passed. In his hands he held a square piece of plywood which he placed on top of cinderblocks that stood vertical on the sidewalk. After making certain it was steady, he set down plastic milk crates on each side of the makeshift table to be used as chairs. Without words he motioned for me to sit and join him for dinner; two strangers on the street sharing Iftar. For the briefest of moments, he disappeared inside only to return with a whole chicken roasted with root vegetables. He placed the pan in the center of the table, took a seat, and began to tear the meat apart with his fingers, motioning for me to do the same. For a moment I watched him eat, knowing that his offer of Iftar strips away any and all ability to say no, for food is how we connect; these shared meals are what unite us in an ever-dividing world. To him it did not matter what religion I was, where I was from, or what I was doing in Amman. All that mattered was that I was hungry, and he had food. I do not know how to say I am a 'vegetarian' in Arabic, so I said nothing at all; chicken has never tasted so good.

Soon we were joined by his cousins who were more than ready to break their fast. They laughed at their

71

young cousin for finding an American and even more so when I had used up all the Arabic words I could speak except for one. Before departing on this journey, *zawj* was one of my favorite words in Arabic. I love the hardness of its beginning and the softness of its end. The word is simple. It means husband. As in:

"Where is your husband?"

This question was quickly followed by a second question:

"Where are your children?"

And then the third, asked in a disbelief unheard of since the proposition that the world is not flat, but round:

"You are alone?"

I laughed, unable to explain to these men, so full of bravado and charm, that I was able to keep my own company, and that loneliness did not exist on a journey such as this. Of course, the next question came as no surprise. I had been waiting for it. It is a question that is asked by all men who encounter women who are wild in the world and desire them to be tame:

"Will you marry me?"

It was not asked in the romantic manner that I always imagined that a stranger whose name I did not know and might never see again would propose marriage, but rather he proposed via Google translate. But it was asked in earnest and then asked again for good measure. He was strong, handsome, and persistent and for a moment I contemplated his question because perhaps he might have been serious, but so early in my pilgrimage I was not ready to commit to anything other than dinner and so I declined, regretfully, his offer of both his hand and more food for I felt it unfair to take one and not the other. Still hungry, I walked away from what could have been true love.

There is a restaurant in Amman so famous that it is said that even the King of Jordan dines there from time to time. Long after the crowds dispersed I arrived alone and asked for a table for one, but tables like this do not exist in Jordan and before another step was taken into the restaurant I was invited to sit at a table full of food and men. The owner called to me from across the restaurant:

"You sit here. You sit with us."

Again, it was impossible to say no.

The dishes were deep and brimming with meat and peppers, lamb and rice. I sat among men speaking Arabic, English and even just a little bit of Spanish. When the men had had their fill, they pushed their chairs away from the table and lit cigarettes, the first of the day for many. Away from the crowd, they took long drags as if having forgotten this simple pleasure and wanting to remember once more.

When the food had grown cold and the night had grown quiet, I took my leave of them, thanking them for their kindness and promising to one day return to this table. As I walked back to the hotel, with both my heart and my stomach full, I wondered what it is I should do with all this kindness. But that is the thing about kindness. It cannot be kept. It must be passed on.

Early the next morning I hired a driver. He arrived smartly dressed in grey slacks and a grey button-down shirt with a mustache closely trimmed above his lip. He spoke softly with an English accented by the desert and the dust. It was just the two of us. Quietly, we went into the desert to visit castles made of sand, which rise like from nothing, and to nothing they will return. We drove through the barren landscape passing signs along the highway indicating that Iraq was just kilometers away. I wondered what it would be like to keep driving east into a country ravaged by war and invaded by my country because of their apparent possession of weapons of mass destruction, but we stayed in Jordan as did my dreams of visiting a country said to be the cradle of civilization.

From the desolation of the rocky plains rose small tornadoes, circular gusts of wind, lasting for no more than a moment before settling again into the sand. It was a beauty so raw that it made me question whether or not it was real; a reality swiftly returned to when war planes, invisible in the sky were heard flying eastward towards Syria, towards war, towards destruction, but they disappeared before they were seen, which made me wonder what else could be made disappear in this desert.

As we drove, Azraq refugee camp came into view. In operation since 2014, Azraq is now home to 32,000 Syrian refugees who have pored over the borders of Jordan to escape from the seemingly never-ending violence in Syria. I looked back as we passed only to see rows of houses and tents so neatly in a line that they look everything but temporary. They look as permanent as war.

When we arrived at Qasr Kharana, the first of the desert castles, there was no one there. Even the guard could not be found. For six weeks I had walked through a world full of crowds and now there was no one to speak to, there was no one to see. Alone, I climbed to the top of the castle walls, past barriers and signs written in Arabic and English warning of the dangers of such a climb, but knowing that I may never pass this way again, I reached higher until there was no higher to go and all that there was beyond the walls was desert; a sky empty of clouds, a land empty of life.

The day, like the desert, expanded before us and we visited Qasr Amra, a castle built by Walid Ibn Yazid, an Umayyad caliph of the eighth century known for his love of poetry and beautiful women. It is the most famous of the desert castles, decorated with frescoes over a thousand years old. Inside and alone a young and bold Bedouin man entered and placed his hands on either side of my hips, pressing himself against me. A hint of this morning's cigarette, both stale and sweet, lingered upon his breath as he spoke ever so softly about my two greatest loves: history and art. Leaning closer, he pointed to the frescoes in various stages of restoration and conservation on the walls and the ceilings.

"There, do you see the king?" I nodded ever so gently, fearful that any grander movement might invite more on his part.

"Can you see the gifts that have been brought before him?"

"Do you want to get closer?"

"Do you want me to get closer?"

I am certain that there are other things that he might have liked to point out as well for he spoke with the assured confidence of man that left no doubt that these tricks have worked for him before. Now I could have turned around and offered him all the things that he wanted, surrendering to his desires and maybe even my own, but I did not. Not here. Not now. I will not be this type of tourist. We exited, blinded by the glare of the sun. Determined still he pressed and invited me back into the desert that night to see the stars, but it was apparent from the way he looked at me and not up at the sky that his idea of stars and mine were not the same and I politely told him no.

When the afternoon grew late and the shadows of the sun grew long, we returned to Amman so that my guide could be home in time to break his fast. When the sun began to slip quietly from the sky, I went again to the Roman ruins to watch it fall. Everything was pink and the heat was visible, like fire burning in the distance. As I scrambled to the top of a concrete barrier a woman called out to me in English that there was another place I can go for an even better view. Gazing across the city I wondered where could be better than this, but she knew more than I, so down I climbed to hear what advice she had to offer. She wore a black hijab that matched her black business suit. In her right hand she held a briefcase and in her left two plastic bags filled with Styrofoam containers. Seeing that sun no longer hung in the sky, she invited me to join her and her daughters for Iftar. It was a meal of chicken and French fries, which we ate with our fingers as they told about their lives in Jordan. She is a lawyer who has her own practice in Amman. In between bites she nudged her young daughters to practice their English, but they were hungry and shy and probably felt the same way as I did when I was their age and my mother struck up a conversations with strangers: that their mother was crazy. But years have a funny way of turning us into our mothers and I was grateful to this mother for being crazy enough to not only speak to me, but to share this small meal with a stranger.

Only a day in the desert and it had stolen my heart. Not wanting it back anytime soon I rented a car to explore more of it, zigzagging the country in search of more ruins, more castles, mountains, and the sea. I was hesitant to drive in Jordan. If the roads were anything like those in Lebanon I was out of my element where lanes, blinkers, and speed limits are only options and not laws. These roads are also home to the most random speed bumps in the world that appear without warning and disappear all the same. As it was, this rental was not equipped with the best brakes in the world and it might have been in the best interest of the entire car had the tires been replaced miles ago, hundreds of miles ago. The interior smelled of cigarettes and the air-conditioner was as reliable as a snowstorm in the desert in the middle of July, but it started with a turn of a key and the radio carried the tunes of Bing Crosby and Dean Martin across the desert sands and here I was, an American woman driving in a foreign land participating in one of the greatest expressions of freedom there ever was: driving on an open road.

I drove so far north to Umm Quais that any further and I would no longer be in Jordan. The first to arrive at the closed gates of the ancient city, I parked my car and entered with the men who work among the ruins. They carried with them shovels and hoes and one even pushed a wheelbarrow. When the path diverged, we parted ways. Then, it was a strange juxtaposition to walk all alone, except for Shepherds tending their sheep, along the cobblestoned streets of an acropolis thousands of years old; the colonnades crumbling, the amphitheater still intact. It was strange to walk through history like a ghost. Every now and again a noise broke the silence. It was hard to ignore even though I had never heard the sound before. It boomed in the distance. Too far to be afraid, to close to be ignored.

And then the realization;
My steps slowed.
My heart stopped.

I stood as still as can be on top of this mountain, in this land said to hold so much promise. When I turned my back to the sun, I could see Israel. When I turned my back to the sun, I could hear Syria. And in these moments, with my back turned toward the sun, it was difficult to tell the difference between what were shadows and what was light. I left as quietly as I arrived, stumbling out of the gates as I departed. How difficult it is to walk on two feet while trying to carry all the pieces of a broken heart.

With hours still left in the day I traveled to Jerash, a city said to have been founded by Alexander the Great in 331 B.C. In the first century of the Common Era it entered Roman influence, as seen in the architecture of its colonnaded streets and the majesty of its triumphal arches. But by Jerash I had lost count of columns and I walked down streets of broken cobblestones listening to the caws of crows echo down empty corridors. The sun swept over the fallen city casting shadows over the temples of fallen gods. In need of more shade I sat in the recess of an amphitheater and closed my eyes, imagining what Jerash was like at the height of its glory: what sounds may have been heard where now is silence, what scents would arise from the streets when now there is only dust, what tales would be told. I kept my eyes closed dreaming of the yesterdays that I would never know. I left with the thought that all is impermanent. Even this.

Again, the next morning, I sought the freedom of desert roads. In the distance rose Kerak Castle, standing as it has stood for hundreds of years on top of a mountain. Formidable in size, even from so far away, it is one of the largest crusader castles built in all the Levant. Originally called Crac des Moabites it was a crusader stronghold under Raynald of Chatillon until Saladin, the first Sultan of Egypt, captured it along with his head in 1189. Since then it was a strategic location for the Ottoman Empire and is now a UNESCO World Heritage Site.

It was surprising how easy it was to get lost even in sight of my destination. All the roads seemed to move away from the castle and not toward it. After circling around the city for the second time, still no closer, I pulled to the side of the road and asked for directions from a man who stood outside of his shop. Sensing my frustration, he offered his young son and his friends to be my personal escorts to the castle. In want of adventure they piled into the car, all three in the front, taking turns telling me in Arabic to turn left, right, and to keep straight, giggling the whole time as if this was the funniest thing in the world. When we finally arrived at Kerak, I tipped my valiant guides for their troubles and off they ran, laughing back down the hill.

And then I was, alone, about to enter this fortress and in an incredible twist of fate I had it all to myself to explore for hours in search of secrets said to be hidden there. Shamelessly I am a believer in theories that others dismiss as conspiracies. Throughout the castle I searched high and low for secret passageways and tunnels that speak of the roots of free masonry, but nothing was remained. When I gave up my search for things that did not want to be found, I climbed to the top of the ramparts that crumbled under the desert sun. All that separated me from the land beyond was a sheer drop of the cliff face that Kerak Castle is built upon. Standing triumphant on the edge of the world, I looked everywhere but down. At noon, the call to prayer came from across the desert. It rose and fell with the wind that carried it across the sand momentarily filling the emptiness with its song. When the call ceased, a group of students arrived. It was time to leave. I was alone no more.

After, I drove east to the Dead Sea. The road was so open that there was no other choice but to drive fast, or as fast as possible without worrying if the brakes were going to fail or the tires would fall off. In the space between earth and sky the sea came into view, shimmering turquoise and white against pale pink stones. Still Ramadan, the night was warm and quiet, and the sun set over the land west: Israel. It seemed so close yet so far away. There I would be soon enough, in the heart of Jerusalem, with my mother by my side.

In the early hours of the day I waded into the Dead Sea, weightless, adrift, and silent, staying for what seemed like hours listening to nothing but the sound of the rise and fall of my breath and the beating of my heart. And in that silence, I asked to be healed by these waters for sometimes it is best to pour salt in our wounds; it is what preserves us, it is what makes us strong.

Before returning to Amman a smaller pilgrimage was made to the River Jordan. The parking lot and the baptismal site were several kilometers away from one another and it was not until we passed a military outpost that I understood the distance. There is a dirt path that winds its way from where it is believed that Jesus was baptized to where the river now retreats. In the shade of a canopy that did nothing to hide the heat, I sung softly the song that echoed in my ears since arriving in this holy place. As I caught sight of the river, the border between Jordan and Israel, I sang ever louder, even if only to myself, slipping off my shoes and letting my feet dangle in the shallow water, my toes touching the muddy bottom. It was a song sung by Michael Jackson and now I sung it quietly to myself:

> *But they told me*
> *A man should be faithful*
> *And walk when not able*
> *And fight till the end*
> *But I'm only human.*

Here in Jordan there were few visitors, but across the way, in Israel, there were many. There to be baptized. There to be saved. They were dressed in white robes and surrounded by men with guns, semiautomatics that hung by their waists, their fingers close to the trigger. Watching them I wondered what had become of holiness, for here the line between sacred and profane was narrower than the river that divided us. I stayed silent on my way back to the car and then drove with the windows down and the radio off all the way back to Amman. The next day would lead me back into the desert; how difficult it was becoming, once seen, to leave these sands.

An ill-prepared explorer, I arrived at Petra on an empty stomach and with water bottles that would draw even the most optimistic toward pessimism. This was improper planning on my part, but then again, had I not intentionally chosen to be in the Middle East during Ramadan? Was this experience not part of the journey as well? Was I not aware, most days of my life, what a privilege it is to know where my next meal was to come from? But as luck would have it, the stalls outside of the gates were open and I entered this ancient Nabataean city, still as unprepared as ever, with two liters of water and a handful of nuts.

For the second time on this journey I wished for my father. He was the one that introduced me to Petra when I was a child through the pages of *National Geographic.* He was the one who let me do back flips off his pick-up truck and taught me how to dive under waves just before they crashed. Had he not hoped one day his daughter would find herself exploring far-away lands like he once did? But almost two months had passed, and we still had not spoken, we barely even said goodbye. After all, what good are conversations when you are unwilling to listen to what the other person has to say?

Now I am a stubborn woman and when I arrived in Petra, I wanted nothing to do with the Bedouin men who offered me their horses and their chariots to see the famed treasury. And so, I veered left, away from the beaten path and nowhere near the treasury at all. I do stupid things like this; allow the bull in my head and the lion in my heart to guide me. There was barely a trail, only small cairns indicating which direction to take. Scrambling up the boulders, I imagined what the phone call to my mother would be like: "Your daughter has disappeared in the deserts of Jordan." But if I was to disappear, at least I was to disappear happy.
It was within those first hours in the desert that I entered the desert of my own soul, the empty places of my heart where nothing can hide, not even my doubts or my insecurities, my pride or my stubbornness. And this emptiness confronts you like the heat, weighing heavy on

your heart, leaving you only two choices: to hold on or to let go.

Before the water ran dry and there were no more nuts temples carved from sandstone came into view. I was lost no more. Emerging from the rocks I stumbled into a young Bedouin who had just unhitched his camel. His long hair was tucked under a red bandana and his khaki cargo pants hung loosely around his waist. An unlit cigarette hung from his lips and it stayed where it was even though his mouth opened into a wide smile when he first caught my glance. With eyes that saw the world as it is, not as he wants it to be, he looked not at me, but through me and I immediately found peace in his presence. It was as if we were old friends who had arranged to meet at this very place, at this very time, and on this very day. His name was Khaled and we walked side by side as his camel kept pace with our steps, even though Khaled did not walk so much as saunter. Our talk grew as big as the world and we dived straight into all of it: capitalism, imperialism, and the long shadows of history. I only have patience for conversations such as this.

To escape from the heat that had caused my fingers to swell and my knuckles to turn white, we found shelter in a cave lined with faded carpets, hard pillows and colorful blankets. Once inside, the temperature dropped and we were joined by Khaled's friend, Emad. In a quiet corner, made all the quieter because it was just the three of us, Emad and Khaled lit cigarettes for one another and we continued our conversation. We talked about politics and religion; we may have even spoken about sex: that holy trinity of topics that no one is supposed to talk about in polite company, but it would have been rude not to speak of these things. There is so little time in this life for only pleasantries. Soon after, ISIS was mentioned. In Jordan, they call them Daesh:

83

those who sow discord and all along my journey there was not one man, woman, or child that I met that did not speak ill of these people and not condemn them as cowards and not Muslims at all.

Would that we could all allow ourselves to have conversations like this everywhere we went so that our eyes, our hearts and our minds may open for countries may be different, divided as they are by borders, but the conversations are always the same. Everywhere in the world there is good and there is bad, but mostly there is good; a good that transcends boundaries of race, sex, age, and religion. There is enough good to give one hope.

As the light slowly retreated from the day, I left Khaled and Emad to finally seek out the Treasury, the most famed building in all of Petra, which is only a facade and no more. The road was carved by rocks whose colors changed with the hours and finally reaching the treasury, I sat in front of it until shadows cast across the stones, hiding the light and revealing the darkness.

The next morning Joanne, my girl from Beirut, came to Petra and off we set with Khaled and Emad into to explore mountains the desert. There we wandered for hours talking about everything and nothing at all. This was where Emad and Khaled grew up and this is where they will grow old. When the height of the sun could go no higher, we stopped for coffee at the monastery, drinking deeply from paper cups, the hot liquid cooling our warm bodies more than the shade we found ourselves under.

Unwilling to end the day when the sun went down, they invited Joanne and I to sleep not at our hotel but under the desert moon. Never wanting to be contained by walls we accepted. We drove into the darkness and set up camp on a sandstone shelf; high enough from the ground to be safe and low enough not to be scared. As the embers of the fire faded into midnight, we fell asleep under the stars, somewhere in the middle of quiet conversations, the moon pregnant in the sky.

Day broke spreading its fractured rays of pink across the desert. Then rose the heat, stripping from the night what relief it had offered and when it arrived, we rolled up the bedding and drove to Khaled's house. In his kitchen we scrambled eggs, diced tomatoes, and boiled water for tea. When everything was prepared, we sat in a circle and ate with our hands, laughing as if this was not the first time that we shared together a night in the desert. The morning grew late and we said our goodbyes hoping that one day we would all find one another in this ancient place once more.

By Wadi Rum, it had been forty days without rain.

On her way back to the Red Sea, Joanne dropped me off on the side of the road in the middle of the desert. Moments later I was picked up by a young man who was a guide from the Bedouin camp that Joanne recommended I stay at while in Wadi Rum. He was no older than twenty, but his eyes and skin already hinted of a life lived in the unforgiving landscape of the desert. Through the empty expanse we drove, windows down and the radio loud over sand and into the depths of the desert; a wilderness so bare that it emptied all thoughts only to fill them again and again. The sun was already at unimaginable heights spreading its heat like fire across the sand. Here there are no structures made by man, only mountains carved by the wind and if you stand silent you can feel the sea, as if this was not a desert but the very bottom of an ocean floor without an ocean above.

At the camp there was a young French woman who had come to the desert weeks before and never left. Together we lounged in what shade could be found. It was hot, too hot to move, to think, to speak and so we sat in endless stillness and silence waiting for the sun to shift, to sink, to do anything other than shine. Hours later, maybe only moments, Ahmed, the Bedouin who ran this camp with his brother, arrived in robes of white contrasting from the dark hair that fell upon his shoulders. He was a striking figure with a pronounced nose and a height that only knew what it was to stand tall. Immediately I was drawn to him sensing his intelligence, his quiet strength, and his solitude. He spoke English in an accent that told of many teachers. In words that hinted sometimes of a British influence and other times French or German, he spoke softly, almost in a whisper, of his life both within and beyond the desert. It took him all but a minute to convince me to take a ride with him into the empty expanse of Wadi Rum. He knew this place. He knew of its secrets; which ones to share and which to keep. We drove into the nothingness and I listened to him as I gazed out the window, blinded by beauty both barren and brimming with life. Barefoot we climbed along the edges of rocks to the place where water collects after the rain. Higher we went, the stones hot and smoothed by the wind until we came to rest in one of the wadis that give Wadi Rum its name. Ahmed threw a rock down a narrow crevasse and we waited in silence until we heard the unmistakable splash of solid hitting liquid, and then, as if having proven that water can still be found in the desert he turned on his heels and led the way out.

After we drove slowly over sand that shifted under the weight of the truck, staying in low gear as the desert landscape opened and closed before us. We stopped briefly at a small stone structure, the stone walls crumbling, the roof long gone. Curious, I asked Ahmed what this was. Indignant, he rolled his eyes before responding with a hint of anger in his voice:

"This is where T.E. Lawrence used to live."

He did not care to elaborate, and I knew enough about history not to ask anymore questions. We left as quietly as we arrived, never looking back to see the former home of Lawrence of Arabia slowly being swallowed by the sands.

To break the silence, Ahmed began to tell a story. I had heard it before from Joanne but wanted to hear it again; this time from his lips. He laughed before he began. How could he ever forget his first encounter with a white man? He must have been eight years old, maybe less, herding his camels through the desert. Superstitious and alone with his older brother he feared what many Bedouin children fear in their youth: jinn, those mysterious creatures of Arabic folklore said to possess a cunning magic. It might have been early in the morning, or maybe it was the middle day when they stumbled upon a small object the likes of which the two of them had never seen before: a tent made not from the hides of goat and camel but from nylon and metal. Crouching low to the ground they readied their guns, rifles that were as tall as they. I imagined them taking aim at all their fears: jinn, death, and the world beyond this desert. How scared they must have been. How excited. They counted to three before pulling their triggers, creating large holes in the fabric where just moments before there were none. From the top of a mountain they heard a scream so loud that to this day it still echoes across these sands. Still fearful, they aimed their guns higher, towards the source of this commotion and trained their barrels on what they thought to be their jinn with skin the color of clouds, eyes the color of the sky, and hair the color of the sand beneath their feet. But they did not shoot for the jinn, he surrendered, and Ahmed and his brother led him back to their camp to show their father the prize they now possessed. Their father suppressed a smile when they returned with their prisoner, informing his sons that this was no jinn; just a lone white man camping in the desert, happy to have been out of his tent and not in when these young boys decided to set their childish fears at ease. I wanted to hear this story again and learn more of what it is like to grow up in a world where imaginations run free, but we became as quiet as the desert and drove back to camp; this time Ahmed bringing with him a white woman instead.

The world spun slowly away from the sun and I sat alone atop of rocks that know both of harshness and softness, that know nothing and everything of time. The wind lifted, creating another small tornado that lasted no more than a moment, but still long enough to arouse me from my reverie. In this awakening I gathered a handful of sand and allowed it to slip through my fingers, watching each grain fall, like civilizations, back to the earth. As the last grain fell to the ground, I remembered that my time, too, will come to an end and to this sand I will return.

When nothing remained of the light I descended from the rocks, still emanating heat from a day of fervor and fire. In the center of the camp there were huts, each with two beds and a light bulb that hung from the ceiling. But within those walls I did not sleep. I could not allow my dreams to be contained or confined in so small a space. Instead I went back to the rocks to lay under a sky full of stars, trying to count every one, but I fell asleep long before the seven sisters of Pleiades could be named.

The first rays of light scattered from the east, its shadows shortened and lengthened across the sand and another day was spent hiding from a merciless sun. Among the rocks, teacups were filled and emptied, only to be filled again and what conversations were had lasted but for a moment before returning to the silence. When the sun too had enough of the day Joanne returned to spend the night in the Valley of the Moon. After dinner we walked into the sands without end. The moon was full, guiding us deeper into the depths of the desert, and we wondered what it would be like to stay here and never return to the world we had known before this; but to stay or to leave, which is worth exploring more?

In the hours before midnight the Bedouin men crowded around the fire and sang us to sleep their lullabies of the Levant. The flames danced and the light disappeared into the shadows. Eventually my eyes did close and I slept the sleep of one thousand and one nights; the full rose moon my pillow, the stars my blanket, and the wind a thousand and one kisses in the darkness. Morning came as slowly and as quietly as the night and the light returned long before the rising of the sun. And like the slow coming of day my thoughts turned slowly to this:

If this life offers me love, not in the form of a lover, but
rather peace in this place of both silence and space,
then happily will I return to the arms of this desert and
allow my heart to grow still.

On my last day in the desert I drove with Ahmed back to Petra. Despite the heat I rolled down the window and leaned on its edges, wanting to memorize this landscape knowing that every day it alters, erasing everything but memories, even mine, but like dust it settles into your heart where forever it stays calling you back, back, back, to the first empty spaces you called home.

On the highway we spoke of then and now and all the time in between. The truck climbed one last hill and then Petra came into view and we descended into the city. As we waited, the car idled and we leaned into one another, so much so that our foreheads almost touched, and I had to edge even closer just to hear him speak. Captivated, I waited in silence for what words traveled from his thoughts to his lips. He lit a cigarette and recited the first verse of the Quran. By now I have heard it so often that I was embarrassed not to be able to repeat it back to him. But I listened as he said it first in Arabic and then in English. Sometimes these sound like the only words in the world.

Still Ramadan, the sun stood high. I hungered and I thirst, but this, too, could wait. We returned to the desert and rather than staying another night among crowds, Ahmed, in need of solitude, went alone to seek refuge in the only place his heart has ever known. When it was time to say goodbye, we embraced and his lips, more full than last night's moon, graced mine. It was brief enough to believe that it did not happen and then, like a thief unwilling to get caught after having stolen this kiss, a kiss I would have freely given, he disappeared into the desert; a mirage of a man, a Bedouin to the bone.

In the morning we were driven to Aqaba by a Bedouin whose years had taken the black from his hair only to replace it with grey and the lines around his eyes spoke of a life lived under a harsh and wild sun. From the mountains to the sea he said more with his silence than any words that have ever escaped my lips. With us there was a young American from the Midwest; one of the very few Americans that I had encountered thus far on my pilgrimage. He was quiet, but when he spoke it was not with softness and I was reminded of all the things that I had left behind.

"I knew not to trust THESE people," he said with a grimace as he lifted his bag from the bed of the truck. I imagined how heavy it must have been for him to carry his fears with him all the way to Jordan. Maybe he did not know that when he packed his bags that he should have left his fear behind for his fear only served to weigh him down. Their infraction was simply a miscommunication as to what hotel he was to be dropped off at in Aqaba. Something easily remedied for the cost of a few words. But he stayed silent. Joanne rolled her eyes and for a moment our faces mirrored one another's. She, too, is a Virgo, and our intolerance for intolerance is strong. Saying nothing to him, we thanked Emad and said goodbye without giving this American a second glance. Sometimes distance does so little to soothe the strife in our souls.

Only a night in the desert and Joanne was eager to see the sea again and we spent our day snorkeling in the waters between Jordan, Egypt and Israel. That night we shared our last meal together, full of all the things that we ate in the first and then some more for good measure. I woke before the sun as Joanne slept. How do you say goodbye when it is not known when you will see one another again? It was difficult to say goodbye to Jordan, too, not knowing if or when I was to return, for it was in Jordan, this land of fever, keeper of eternity, that more peace was found.

But to know of peace, one must also learn of war.

THE LAND OF BROKEN PROMISES

From other travelers were heard stories about the Israeli border: crossings that took hours, even whole days where entire bags were emptied, personal possessions confiscated, stolen, and reassigned to a new Israeli owner, and uncomfortable and invasive questions were asked.

It was with these worries, just after the rising of the sun, that I climbed into a cab that took me to the border between Jordan and Israel. With hesitation I walked to the gates that divided one country from the other, fearful of leaving a land to which I might never return and even more fearful to enter another. Prepared for an inquisition I erased all the messages from my friends and even what notes there were on my phone about Lebanon and Jordan, paranoid that it might be held against me in this new land. Some may regard these as unnecessary measures, but I felt their necessity. I did not want to explain to my mother that not only was I not allowed into Israel, but worse yet, I would not be able to meet her in a few days. And yet, after only five minutes, I was waved through and rather than a stamp on the passport a small piece of paper, no bigger than my thumb, was slipped between its pages, the only proof of passing through this land.

Once free from the border, dinars were exchanged for shekels and another cab was taken to the bus station in Eliat. There were hours before the next bus north to Mitzpe Ramon was to arrive, where I was to spend the next few days hiking and exploring the desert. To escape from the inescapable heat, I sat in the shade, shoulders bare, shorts above my knees, drinking coffee and eating a croissant, publicly and in broad daylight for the first time since Ramadan began. Had I known this was to be my first and last sense of freedom that I was to experience in Israel, I may have lingered longer on this bench.

The bus arrived promptly at its designated hour and we stood in line to board. It was a Sunday and children made soldiers half of my age were returning to their bases after a weekend away, each with a patch sewn onto the sleeve of their uniform, insignia indicating what branch they formed in the military. Having lived in a city with an army base, the sight of a soldier in uniform was not new to me, but something was different here, more ominous. And thus, began an unease that I was unable to shake for the ten days I spent in Israel.

Before boarding the bus, the soldiers stored their bags in the compartment below, but they kept their rifles with them, laying them carelessly across their laps as if they were mere accessories and not the weapons that they are. It was a sight so jarring in its casualty that I had to look away and so I stared out into the stark reality of the desert searching for signs of life, but there were none: no trees, no water, only a heat that lingered like death in the air.

Base after base we stopped. There were so many that I lost count after four. At each, soldiers disembarked, carrying with them their weapons that were never intended for peace. As we drove my mind drifted back to the lands that I left behind and the hospitality with which I was welcomed to the Levant and how quickly that hospitality was exchanged for hostility in this land; a hostility so apparent that I crept to the edges of my seat, crossing my legs and arms in order to protect myself from what harm may come. Some may regard this as an overreaction, a dramatic response to a culture different from my own, but for years I had denied traits that should never be neglected: intuition, instinct, and empathy. Ignoring them in the past had only gotten me into trouble, but now, at thirty-six years old, I had come to rely on these senses for they are what keep me out of the arms of harm. Because of this I knew, only hours entering Israel, that if my mother was not to meet me in Jerusalem, I would have left as soon as I arrived.

Three hours and countless stops later we arrived at Makhtesh Ramon, a town on the edge of a crater that extends in all directions, reminding the world just how harsh and cataclysmic this universe could be. Late in the afternoon, the sun fell, its light elongating in lines of cracked earth as it descended. The wind screamed and wailed across the expanse. Everything grew cold and black; here the day is the only thing that surrenders, giving way to darkness, to nothingness, to night.

To the Negev I had come to spend more time in the desert. For most of my life, all I had ever known was to be surrounded by the sea and now here was a land that held only promises, but whether those promises have been kept or broken, it was still too early to tell.

I also came to the desert to hike; to wander through the desert as prophets and pilgrims before. Until then hiking for me was only walking. But I still like to consider myself an athlete and these hikes were to be practice for the rest of this journey. Silly me, I even thought that I had broken in my hiking boots before I left, but what are blisters, really, but an opportunity for the body to heal itself?

The alarm rang at half past five. Quietly I dressed and set out into the unknown. The sun rose sharp, like a knife in the sky, dividing the night from the day so severely that the night was all but forgotten with the dawn. Down the crater I walked in staccato steps still uncertain as to what path I was to take. Was it to be a short loop skirting the edge or a long trek across the center? I chose the latter and my journey into nothingness began.

The sun and the heat rose by degrees. From the depths of the desert a sound breached the silence. It was the same that was heard in Umm Quais only louder and closer. Again, my steps slowed, or did they quicken? How does one walk when listening to an entire nation practice for war? Unable to ignore this noise that now could not be mistaken for any other, my steps began to land like thunder, matching the beat of my heart. Boom. Boom. Boom. For nineteen kilometers I walked through the desert. Nineteen kilometers of sun without shade, air without wind, and stifled and bated breath. Eventually I emerged from the crater and hitchhiked back to the hostel, the car silent, my thoughts deafening.

I arrived in the Eternal City the day before my mother and waited for her there. Her plane was to land in the morning, and we were to spend a week with one another. This was to be part of the pilgrimage that we shared together. We had chosen Israel because she had raised me Italian and Catholic and most of our Sundays were spent at mass listening to the scriptures of the saints and letters from the apostles. Always rebellious, I doubted the church and its teachings as much as my mother believed in them. But we had found common ground on the spiritual side of faith where one is led by the heart and not through the testaments.

That afternoon I went to a café to participate in one of my most favorite pastimes: drinking coffee and watching the world pass by. The tables were small with marble tops the color of marble and slate and the wicker chairs had geometric patterns that matched the tiled floor. From the speakers wafted the voice of Edith Piaf, the Sparrow. For the shortest of moments, I thought that maybe I was in Paris and not Jerusalem, but then the undeniable sound of Hebrew was heard across the table. It came from an Israeli woman, young, vibrant, and reckless as only youth can be. She was commanding her friend across from her to lean closer as she lifted her phone up higher to take the perfect picture. Between them were profiteroles, but they barely noticed the ice cream was melting, creating a pool of cream-colored liquid on their plate. When the right angle could not be found they politely asked for me to take their picture and then they introduced themselves. Sarah was quiet and modest, but Yasmine moved like a whirlwind, as if when she stopped, her whole world would collapse around her. Some move like cyclones without ever knowing that people, too, can be tornadoes, unaware of the destruction they leave in their wake.

In the ever-rising heat of the late afternoon the three of us went to the Israel Museum so close to closing that it was a drive by visit. Through the corridors we ran past antiquities, old masters, and modern men. We even came upon an installation by Chinese artist Ai Weiwei, whose very presence in this place struck me as out of place. Did he not know what it means to be imprisoned in the land of his birth? We stayed for only a short while before being kicked out, pursued off the grounds by a guard who seemed well practiced in the art telling people that they no longer had the right to be where they were. As we waited for a bus back to the city center Yasmine asked how I was to spend the rest of my time in Israel. When I told her that I would be traveling to the West Bank she scoffed, looked back over her shoulder, and told me in a shrill voice full of fear and terror, that to go there is unspeakable, forbidden, unthinkable and that I should not risk my life for something so foolhardy. Already knowing that her warning would be ignored rather than heeded I wondered if the West Bank was not more dangerous than sitting on a bus full of young men, whose military service was perfunctory, with automatic rifles slung across their laps. I wondered what was more dangerous: to witness or to remain blind to what can all too easily be hidden behind walls. I wondered when it was that unification became more dangerous than separation. And then it struck me: Yasmine was only told one story; she only listened to one story.

We must listen carefully to the stories that we are told for these are the real dangers of this world: allowing lies to become truths and truths to become lies.

The bus arrived and we went our separate ways and I, as always, was grateful to have quiet once again. When shadows grew as long as history I wandered around the old city searching for meaning in the labyrinth of passageways, darkened alleys and flashes of golden light. By the Jaffa Gate I met a Palestinian man who invited me to sit and share with him Arabic coffee and conversation. He lit a cigarette, handing it to me before lighting another, leaning into it with his elbows, the table unsteady, his gaze everything but. He closed one eye as he pulled from the filter, his face aflame with shadows and fire. We smoked, taking long drags from the cigarettes and even longer sips from our coffee as tourists poured into the city. As I ate falafel, we spoke of Palestine and Israel, Jerusalem and Al Quds.

"We do not want war." He said, lighting another cigarette. "We want Palestine. We want peace." And then, in a whisper, "We want our freedom." He took from the cigarette one last drag and then he stubbed it. He did not take another, but the smoke still surrounded him, lingering in the air like words left unsaid. Watching the smoke rise like the walls that surround this city and then disappear, I thought how strange it is that one man's peace is another man's imprisonment.

With him I wanted to stay, but the hour was late, and my mother would soon be here. I thanked him for the kindness of his words and his company. He smiled and took my hands in his, clasping them close. They were soft and warm like his eyes that shined; whether with happiness or sadness, it was difficult to tell. As he let go, he told me to remember this and only this: "What is in your heart is on your tongue."

How can that be something that I will ever forget?

It had been two months since I last saw my mother. She arrived at first light on a non-stop flight from New York. We cried when we saw each other, disbelieving that all the things we had spoken of had come true. Jet lagged, she slept most of the morning, but in the afternoon, we explored Jerusalem. We walked slowly, careful not to miss anything. Never had just the two of us traveled alone together before. Although her first born, fate had placed me in the middle of her children, or the end, depending upon which family tree that is chosen to climb and, unlike the stones beneath our feet, time had yet to smooth the sometimes rough journey together as mother and daughter. But now it was just the two of us and the strength that I had admired in my mother for so long would again called upon for all of the days that followed.

As the sun burned down upon the city, we visited the Dome of the Rock, passing through three security checkpoints and crossing over a wooden ramp built suspended over the ground below. There was a sign that read that, according to the Talmud, it is forbidden for Jews to enter this area. I found this strange because, maybe if it were not forbidden, then perhaps there might be more understanding between Israelis and Palestinians instead of a forced separation between the two. But then again, who am I to enter a country purporting to know the difference between what is right and what is wrong? We, or at least I, entered with a sigh of relief. Finally, here was something familiar. We walked to the doors of the mosque but were barred entrance by a man who stood a foot taller than the two of us.

"I'm sorry, only Muslims are allowed inside."

Forever a New Yorker, my mother leaned into the man standing outside of Qubbat al-Sakhra and asked, "Well, how do you know we are not Muslim?"

And because I am my mother's daughter I added, "Does it count if I am Muslim in my heart?"

He did not answer. He simply stood at the entrance and smiled as we walked away. We stayed for only a little longer and then returned over the wall. For the briefest of moments, I stood suspended between the past and the present wondering how many walls are put up thinking they are to protect us when it is the opposite that is true.

Fifteen minutes they said, not for the first time and certainly not for the last. It was a Friday during Ramadan and we waited for the bus that was to take us from East Jerusalem to the West Bank. Fifteen minutes extended to an hour and that hour slowly became two.

Perhaps here, where lives, like people, are separated by walls, time is just as easily divided and can only be measured in the smallest of increments.

As we waited, we watched as thousands of Palestinians descended upon the Damascus Gate in the hopes of arriving at Qubbat al-Ṣakhrah in time for the midday prayer. They were shuffled through, like cattle, as

102

IDF soldiers, rifles held at the ready, their fingers only inches away from the triggers, flanked them on either side. The adhan wailed and for once this world grew quiet. After, the buses began to arrive, one-by-one, and we clambered aboard and took our place among Palestinians: mothers and daughters, fathers and sons, and children, so many children, and drove in the direction of Bethlehem. It was not far, less than six miles, but it seemed a world away. The bus stopped just steps away from the West Bank and we were let out to join the ever-growing line that formed outside of the gates. Most stood in silence, still uncertain as to how much longer they would be made to wait.

The wall, almost as old as it is tall, rose before us in thick slabs of grey concrete punctuated with watchtowers, barbed wire, and Israeli soldiers dressed in riot gear. My mother cried as we stood in front of the guarded gates. For most of the morning she had attempted to tell me how there were two sides to every story and I could not convince her that those two sides are the side that we have been told and the side that is conveniently kept from view. And still, this was not what she expected. This was more than she feared.

Somehow Apartheid still has a way of surprising us.

When the gates finally opened, with a flash of red lights and the moan of metal separating from metal, we walked into the West Bank, where we were greeted by the shouts of men hoping to sell their fruits, their trinkets, and their toils to the world outside of these walls and the arguing of other men hoping that they will be the ones chosen to be our guide within. It is here, just as the gates closed ever so slowly, long enough for those inside the walls to catch a heart wrenching glimpse of the world outside, that we found Marwan, a young Palestinian taxi driver, and the three of us made our way to his car parked far from the fury.

"Welcome to my big prison," he said as we shut the doors to his black sedan, the windows rolled down, and the radio low. I met his eyes in the rear-view mirror. They are brown like his skin and despite the anger in his words there was a softness in his voice and in his eyes that pleaded with mine: *Look at me. Look at this*. Holding his gaze, I saw that our ages were not far from one another and I sensed that there was no distance in our thoughts. There was no difference in our dreams. He started the car and drove both towards and away from the madness, pointing to all of the tourist attractions along the way:

Here is where Banksy painted his first song of protest.
There is where the angels, they were heard on high.
Here is where Christ the King was born.
There is where they build the illegal settlements.
There is where they have electricity.
There is where they have clean water.
Here is where we sometimes have none.

He stopped on top of a hill that overlooks the land beyond these walls. We climbed out to take in the world in which we found ourselves; a world separated by walls of fear, pain, and collective grief. But we did not stay long. Before shutting the doors, I imagined Marwan here in the darkness waiting for angels, dreaming of freedom, searching for stars.

At the Church of the Holy Nativity there is a door of humility. It stands open, allowing the light of the sun to penetrate even the darkest chambers. To enter you must stoop low and bow your head in prayer. We entered quietly, covering our shoulders and descending the stairs into what might have once been a manger. My mother crouched low to the ground in the small recess of a room

104

adorned with golden frescoes and lit by candlelight. She held her hand on the silver-plated marble floor said to be where the son of God was born, finally realizing all that she believed to be true. And yet, as she reveled in this sacred moment, she was pushed out of the way by a tourist armed with a selfie stick hoping to capture the perfect pose of herself at the birthplace of Jesus Christ.

It was then that something in my spirit shattered and I had to bite my tongue and turn away knowing all too well just how capable I am of doing all of the things that Jesus would not do in a situation like this and for the sake of my mother I did not even though my anger did not subside. It rose in me hot and tempestuous like the desert sun and try as I could to harbor the light, it was the darkness that came for me. But to scream or to remain silent? Sometimes these seem like our only choices.

As the sun began to descend into darkness, Marwan took us back to the gates that remain locked not from within but from without. Bittersweet, we said our goodbyes and he disappeared back into the crowd and we, only there for one day, were able to escape just hours after we arrived, leaving behind Marwan and all who are forced to spend their entire lives behind these walls. We returned to the city lost in thoughts that are thousands of years old.

On our last day in Jerusalem we walked the *Via Dolorosa*, the Way of Sorrow, from the Lion's Gate to the Church of the Holy Sepulcher, stopping at each station of the cross along the way. Not one for religious fervor I sought a quiet place on the steps of the courtyard and waited for my mother while she stayed inside. When she emerged from this sacred site said to be where Christ was crucified and entombed, we moved towards the outskirts of the city, towards Gethsemane. Here, crowds did not gather, and we were left to wander, just the two of us.

The church was near empty, but it was not there that we went. It was to the gardens, to the tree whose roots are two thousand years old, where it is said that Jesus spent the night before his crucifixion in contemplation and accepted his fate. Together we sat, allowing waves of calm to wash over us. Here there was no chaos. Here there was only peace.

Now, I am not a holy woman. My spirituality comes and goes, but here it truly felt that if a man such as Jesus did indeed walk this earth, then surely this was where his last night was spent. After, we climbed to the top of the Mount of Olives and gazed upon Jerusalem just as the last rays of light flickered off the burnished plates of the qubba of Qubbat al Sakhra, a glint of gold, a flash of hope, and then both were gone.

In the last days of our journey together my mother and I went to the Dead Sea; so different on one side than the other. Under a relentless and unforgiving sun, we climbed to the top of Herod's Fortress; now only rubble, a palace with no king. Coming down we spent the afternoon by the sea, lying more in the shade than the sun. Above us, American and Israeli fighter jets, heard before they were seen, soared toward Syria. Superstitious, I shielded my eyes and held my breath until they passed overhead; the way I used to when we drove past cemeteries when I was a kid.

War. Death. Are they not the same?

So as not to feel as if I was suffocating or drowning I went down to float in the cerulean sea, but the water was too warm, too dirty, too full of salt and I exited almost as quickly as I entered, but not before bringing my hands too close to my eyes. In a matter of seconds, I went from sight to blindness, calling out to my mother to save me from the sea once again, which she did, guiding me to showers and reassuring me that everything will be ok. How could she be so certain?

When spring became summer we went to Tel Aviv, having cautious conversations everywhere we went for to say too much we might be accused of things that we are not guilty of and to say too little and we are guilty of remaining silent when it is this silence, like so many other things, that must be broken. There we watched the sunset and tried to make sense of all we experienced

On the morning of her departure we walked to Jaffa, stopping for coffee on our way. As we waited, bumping into one another between counters crowded with croissants and pastries, a young woman brought her bicycle into this already small space as if it was the most natural thing in the world. Hearing our accents and our English she asked where we were from and what we felt about her country. She did not wait for a response before asking another: "Isn't it amazing?" Somehow, she expected my answer to be as enthusiastic as her question.

Perhaps from Tel Aviv she could not see the wall that had been built between the State of Israel and the disputed territories of Palestine.

Maybe, at so early an hour and before her morning coffee, she had yet to have the conversation with a Palestinian cab driver that I had only days before in which he welcomed my mother and I to his big prison, where some days were blessed with electricity and running water and others were not. And maybe she might never have the conversation that I had in Lebanon

107

with another Palestinian man who carries with him papers of an inordinate size that speak neither of citizenship nor a country, but of his lack thereof. Perhaps she might never hear the ache in the voice of a man who longed for a home that he would never ever see.

Maybe, concentrating only on her coffee, she was able to ignore this world that collapses and not expands all around her. Maybe from the height of her bicycle seat she sees the way in which children carry the weight of the metallic world so recklessly across their shoulders as a means of protection and not as I see it: a phenomenon so unnerving that chills run up my spine, my skin crawls and my heart aches.

Maybe, from the freedom of her bicycle she is able to breathe the air that suffocates me here in this place.

These last hours passed as slowly as they did quickly and then my mother had to say goodbye. When she departed I was left alone in a place that I would not have stayed had she not been there, had she not offered her hand to hold to keep me steady and her heart because mine, for those days and the days ever since, had been broken. If it were not for my mother, I would have left had she not given me life once more.

When it was my turn to leave, I did not linger. At the airport a young Israeli girl smiled as she placed a yellow sticker on the back of my passport and wished me a safe journey onward. I tried my best to hide my tears, my contempt, my pain, but once through the metal detector I ran to the bathroom, locked myself in the stall, and collapsed on the floor where I hid until my flight to Istanbul was called. After boarding, I sat on the plane and scrolled through photographs of the past ten days: a desert without end, a sea without life, a prison open only to the air with graffiti along its walls over a decade old that tells the story of a conflict that shows no signs of

108

stopping, grounds of persecution, crucifixion, and ascension in the name of all that is holy transformed into spirituality as spectacle. Able to look no more, I, too, have a question I would like to ask the world:

"Amazing, isn't it?

A Heart That is Whole

By Istanbul it had been sixty-nine days without rain.

Summer stepped in, sweeping the spring away by taking the moments of light from the day and giving them over to darkness. Outside of Ataturk Airport, clouds covered the sky, hiding and revealing the sun. A gentle breeze swept in from the west bringing with it thoughts not of sand but of the sea. Everywhere there were trees; abundant and green, full of promise, full of hope. How different Turkey already was from the country that had just been left behind. So oppressive was Israel, so thick the air, so suffocating the heat that I felt that I had lost my ability to breathe, to move, to think, to do anything other than cry. But here in Turkey I felt that I could breathe once more.

On a bus from the airport we drove through the crowded streets towards the shores of Asia, passing cafes, stores, and sidewalks full of Turks reveling in this long June day. There were so many people that any doubt that I may have had about being alone in Istanbul disappeared in a matter of moments for Istanbul is a city of fifteen million spread across two continents but joined together in a history so rich that not even the falling of an empire could strip the soul from this city. It rushes around you, engulfing you in the past, present, and future all at once.

The hotel was nestled on a quiet street near steps that led to the sea. Ships anchored in its harbor and seagulls flew over their masts, calling out across the continents: you are here, you are in Istanbul. Dolphins even swam in the waters. On land stray dogs lay in the shade of oak trees as the wind rustled the leaves above. Always one for the light I sat in the sun and ordered the first of many cups of Turkish coffee. A young man who worked at the hotel placed a ceramic cup between us, smiling as much with his eyes as with his lips. He smiled as if this is the place from where joy comes. I did not know yet that this is the way that Turks speak to one another without words, but it was as warm and welcoming as the coffee that passed between my lips. A Turkish Delight lay on the saucer, dusted chestnut and rolled in coconut flakes. I did not wait to finish the coffee before taking one sweet small bite. It tasted like Turkey: dense and rich and thick like honey. I took from the cup one last sip. The grinds stayed on the bottom. No fortunes were to be told this day. It was all a matter of fate.

In the newfound the freedom of summer I walked toward the ferry that was to usher me from Asia to Europe. As the day brightened, I half skipped, half sprinted, unable to slow my steps as if Newton's second law of physics applied to my legs and feet alone. The scent of the sea lingered in the air, full of salt, full of stories. As the dock grew closer seagulls grew in abundance, crowding the shores with their songs of the sea.

Across the Marmara stood the city: the domes of Aya Sofya, the turrets of the Sultan Ahmed Mosque, and the walls of Topkapi Palace. They seemed even further now that they were so near. Impatient, I climbed up on the small partition that separated the street from the sea and peered over the fence that stood between where I was and where I wanted to be. Had it not been for the things in my pocket that I could not lose, I would have jumped into those blue blue waters and swam to the other side. But I did not. Instead I joined the swelling crowd as it waited for the ferry. When it arrived, I went to the bow and sat on its edge, leaning on the railings to stare at the city, already enchanted by its magic and its might. The engine rumbled as we pushed away from the dock and sunlight tumbled upon the sea, scattering like diamonds across the surface. As we sailed across the Marmara waves rose and fell against the ship, merging and parting in kaleidoscopic crests of cerulean and indigo. Never has a sea been this blue.

It is no small wonder that the word turquoise comes from the work Turkish, as if the color itself was born from these waters.

Momentarily taking my eyes from the city, I turned my gaze to this ship brimming with people, with life. On board the ferry men greeted one another with a clasp of hands and an embrace. Shoulder to shoulder they stood, temples touching as they leaned in close, whispering quiet words that I did not yet understand; an intimacy from which I felt the need to turn away from and yet witness at the same time. Women wearing brightly colored scarves took photographs of their children who climbed the rails of the ferry to throw torn pieces of bread to the seagulls who flew alongside the ship. Rounding the Golden Horn, the place where the Marmara Sea meets the Bosphorus Straight, Galata Tower and its bridge came into view from the east and

Suleymaniye Mosque towered over the western shores. I wanted so much for the ship to stop, for time to stand still, if only for a moment so that I might remember this, but nothing ceased, not the waves, not even the wind.

From the ferry I walked to the center of old Istanbul, Sultanahmet Square; the Mamara coming and going from view as the city sloped upwards. I followed the tracks of the tram around the curves of Divan Yolu past the gates of Topkapi Palace and the Basilica Cistern. When the tram passed, accelerating on the tracks, bells rang, adding to the symphony of Istanbul; a city full of beauty, full of wonder, full of life. Somewhere along the way a man beckoned me inside his restaurant where he poured çayı into a tulip glass and offered small brown stones of sugar to sweeten the hot liquid. I drank from this cup and almost accepted his invitation to come back for dinner, but it was too early to commit to anything just yet. And still I thanked him for his kindness and promised to return one day, a promise I was not certain could be kept.

On the far side of Sultanahmet rose the Jewel of Istanbul, the Blue Mosque with its six blue minarets piercing the too blue sky where everything, the vaulted arcade, the multiplicity of domes, the inlays of marble, is blue. Above the iwans are written verses from the Quran and in the center of the courtyard stands an ablution fountain, the place where Moslems wash themselves before prayers. The mosque was near empty and the few visitors that were there shuffled quietly through the courtyard before disappearing into the many recesses of the mosque. Unable to enter, I left and walked across the square to where my reason for being in Istanbul stood; a building that has haunted my dreams since first learning of its existence. I dreamt of this place, the way one dreams of stumbling upon a great love; knowing that it is out there somewhere, but uncertain if or when it might

115

be found. But there it was. Aya Sofya. A place where two religions do not collide, they coexist. Compared to the Blue Mosque, its structure is simpler, less ornate than its young neighbor, perhaps on account of having been built over a thousand years before. Across the surface of its pink stucco walls spread small cracks, like the lines of a palm, telling the story of Istanbul: its heroes and its villains, its creators and its conquerors. It is a church built for the emperor of Byzantium, Constantine, and then claimed by its conqueror.

I was afraid to enter Aya Sophia, the Church of Holy Wisdom, knowing that I might never want to leave. But still I went, keeping my head down and walking to the center of the room. Only then did I look up and like a dervish I whirled around and around; the golden frescoes blurring in the frenzy. This was ecstasy. This was peace. When finally I stood still long enough to catch my breath I thought that if this breath was to be my very last it would not matter for now, if indeed death were to come for me willingly would I go because I would die happy.

After all, happiness is like death. For both, we do not know what awaits us on the other side.

For hours I stayed within the walls of Aya Sophia, running my hands along the cool marble, tracing the latticework with my fingers, and looking up at the dome, trying to remember the number of times that it had fallen, hoping it would not fall again. Around the edge of the rim hang eight calligraphic roundels on which were written the names Allah, Mohammed and his descendants. Here there are prophets. Here there is God.

When the doors to the museum would no longer stand open, I exited the basilica and wandered down the

116

streets as the sun's last light danced across the cobbled stones. In the approaching twilight I sat between the mosques waiting for what had become my favorite part of day: the call to prayer, in which time both stands still, and an eternity is passed. When it came it came from Aya Sofya, it came from the Blue Mosque, it came from all the three thousand one hundred and thirteen mosques spread across the city. It came loud and it came quietly, rising like a wave from the heart of Istanbul crashing into my own. If there was a sound made by peace, then surely this is what it would sound like.

I closed my eyes and opened them and closed them again in an attempt to distinguish all that was real from a dream. Somewhere in the middle of this closing and opening I stopped, realizing that this was as close to the truth as I will ever come; a truth that cries out like the wind, like these prayers across the city:

You will pass this way only once. Only once. Only once. So, keep your eyes open. Keep your heart open. This is how the light comes in.

Thereafter, these were my days: morning runs along the Marmara followed by bold cups of Turkish coffee, and the writing of every memory, every word. When my hand grew tired and my feet grew restless I walked in all directions hoping to get lost, even though there is no getting lost in Istanbul; there is only discovering what might have been missed had the wrong turn not been taken. This is how I fell in love with Istanbul: one step at a time.

117

Days passed and yet there were things of which I never tired, like the crossing of the sea. Always, I stayed on the bow of the ship watching clouds part and converge in the summer sky. Out on the edge I waited for the call to prayer to rise over the sound of the engine that carried me across the Bosphorus from one continent to another. Often, I found myself leaning against the rails of the ship, resting my chin on top of my hands, and allowing the wind to pass through me, warm and wistful like a much sought after kiss that is remembered no matter how many years may have passed. Sometimes before and sometimes after I would buy a simit, that sweet circular bread that is found on nearly every corner in Istanbul, and eat it as I moved among Turks, visiting bazaars and fortresses, museums and mosques.

From both sides of the street men called from their carpet shops and cafes to all the tourists who passed. They shouted in every language they knew until the right words were said but walking past them it was ever so obvious that they wanted to sell so much more than the objects that spilled from their doors. To sweeten the deal, they also offered Turk kahvesi and dates of all varieties. Of course, they were offering more warmth than that cup could provide and dates that might have turned out to be just pits and nothing more. But they were handsome and determined and everyday it grew harder to say no. Besides, how I do love to flirt.

Less than a week in Istanbul and I felt like flirting, so I wandered through the streets of Istanbul, looking for trouble. He saw me long before I saw him, staring as he did with his Ottoman eyes. Tall and lean, his skin was dark, his hair darker. He came close as he spoke, speaking as if knowing me was an inevitability, a fate that cannot be avoided. For the first time in what seemed an eternity I welcomed a man into my space without cringe and without recoil; a habit picked up years before that I had yet to put down in fear of heartbreak, perhaps even in fear of love. And still he persisted. In the middle of the afternoon, he was on a break from his work and he coyly leaned in to ask:

"Is two hours enough?"

I laughed as he said it, which only made him lean closer and ask again. It did not matter how many times he had used this line on other women. Twice was enough for me.

In our first two hours together, we went for tea. There was a couch in the corner of the café with room enough for many, but we sat close, our knees touching, our eyes never wavering from the other's gaze. In our hands we held small glasses and drank from the warm liquid on this sweet summer day. His name was Celal and he told me of his life before he came to Istanbul, of his time in the army, and his family who still lived in the east. As promised, we stayed together for two hours. Apparently, it was not enough.

Just days later we went out on a midnight date; a dinner so late no one else was there. Far from the Istanbul of bright lights and tourists we shared a bottle of Turkish wine, as soft and light in the body as it was on the tongue. Soon a whole fish arrived, and we pulled it apart with our fingers and let the juice run down our chins and wrists. This meal was not clean, but then again nothing ever is. Cigarettes lay on the table between us, the lighter placed on top. I took one from the pack and lit it, taking one long drag, watching the smoke rise and disappear into the city, all the while thinking that this was not good for me, none of this was good for me. And still, ever after we shared our days together drinking coffee in the afternoon, beer in the evening, and smoking cigarettes well into the night. We went shopping. He bought me a dress. It was the color of pink roses in early June with an empire waste and a sash that tied in the

119

back. The straps on the shoulders stayed up almost as often as they fell. Buttons ran down the spine and there were even pockets that I could put my hands in as I walked down the broad boulevards of Anatolia. So, in love with this dress was I that I wore it every day. It reminded me of summer. It reminded me of Istanbul.

When the streets emptied of light and darkness filled the hours Celal fed me mussels stuffed with rice and doused in lemon that were bought on the side of the road at 3am, warm and full of brine. He slid them off the shell and into my mouth never waiting for me to finish the first before offering another and then another. In between bites I almost grew as impatient as him for I know no other way that I like to be seduced; how I love to be fed. Often, we stayed awake until the first call to prayer broke the silence of the dawn and in the morning I left him to return across the azure sea.

In July, Esra came to share the room with me. She is a teacher from the west of Turkey. Her hair is as wild as her smile and the whole of her body shook when she laughed, contagious and expansive. I loved her immediately. In the mornings we took coffee together under the shade of Chestnut trees. There she taught me my first full sentence in Turkish: *Bugün hava çok güzel*. Today is too beautiful. These words were said every morning when we first stepped outside for they held what only summer could promise: beauty and heat and hope and longing.

Like Lebanon, everything in Istanbul was too much and again, somehow not enough. Esra and I spent our days apart but early in the evening we found one another again somewhere in Istanbul. Together we walked along the bustling streets of Kadikoy passing antique book shops and the fish mongers selling Lüfer and bonito, levrek and barbunya. The fish lay on ice with their heads and tails still intact, their scales shimmering in the sun. So fresh, so raw, so intoxicating was this market that we wished there was a kitchen where we stayed so that we could make dinner with what lay before us. Instead we crossed the sea to eat pizza at her favorite Italian restaurant in Beyoğlu. For dessert she took me to a bakery famous for its baklava. But it was not from Syria and it was not the same. Just before midnight we drank coffee again at the café that she likes to go to when she comes to Istanbul only to continue our conversation that had already lasted the day. On our way home I spoke aloud some more of the Turkish phrases that she had taught me that evening, calling out *Seni seviyorum* to everyone who passed. She laughed as loudly as the people who heard it before she translated their response to my favorite Turkish phrase: *Ben de seni seviyorum*, I love you too.

With hope I wondered what the world might be like if all of us walked among one another and spoke these words to each other in languages that are not our own.

I was sad to see Esra leave, knowing that in her I had found a friend. But even after Esra left there was no rain. Unwilling to wait any longer for the rains to come I went to a Turkish bath. After all, how could one travel to Turkey and not partake in such a simple pleasure? A small sign above the entrance read Hamman, otherwise the wooden door was unmarked. Hesitantly, I entered, and once inside I stripped down to all but my most private parts.

121

Steam rose hot and swirled in the air of the blue and white tiled room. A ceramic ledge wrapped around its edges and fountains jutted forth from the walls. From their cool waters I splashed my skin and scrubbed my feet, cracked and rough from walking countless miles through deserts and cities, up mountains and down valleys. Pressing my head against the tiles, I closed my eyes, and took long deep breaths from the warm air, holding this breath in want of remembering such a sacred moment.

In the center of the room two women, naked to the waist, gently swayed in the rising heat. In their hands they held wash clothes soaked with water and soap, which they used to bathe the women before them. So gentle their motions, so tender their touch that for a moment I envied the freedom of their bodies and the ease of their movements among strangers.

One of the women called me from my corner, gesturing with her hands to lay down in front of her. She smiled as the Turkish do, pursing her lips and blinking her eyes. She began with my back and shoulders and scrubbed away from me every heartbreak, every disappointment and every woe. Turning over, unflinching, she looked in my eyes and held her gaze as if she knew all my secrets but would never say a word. In words unspoken she asked me to sigh again and again. I cried as she did this hoping that my tears would remain hidden in the steam and the mist. But they didn't and finally, there with a stranger, finally I let peace, like thunder, like lightening, like rain, wash over me. How long after I stayed, I do not know. All that is known is that what was heavy going in was light coming out.

After I walked as if in a dream through the streets of Anatolia, eating a fish sandwich wrapped in paper, the filet thin, the bread thick. I barely whispered a word. When darkness flowed like a river, I took a

122

midnight ferry across the sea. As always, I climbed to the top of the stairs and took a seat at the bow. The boat filled with passengers and patiently we sat under the stars, making wishes on everything that fell from the sky. The wind was warm, the sea was calm and the moon, full only yesterday, began to empty itself once more. As the ferry pushed from the dock, the lights of Europe faded in the distance.

On that perfect summer night, the universe, once so big, collapsed in on itself creating a world on that ferry all its own; a world into which happiness was born. This was the night that I discovered happiness, stumbling upon it slowly. For so long I had denied its existence, even going so far as to declare it boring, but happiness is the furthest thing from boring. Happiness is.

That night, happiness was children, still awake, playing in the laps of their mothers as lovers, young and old, held hands and stole kisses from one another under the moonlight. Happiness was a young man with a guitar plucking each string as if playing for the first and last time. Happiness were the strangers who sang with him, together, as one, and if ever there was any doubt as to whether there was still good in this world it was erased on that July night. Even off the ferry, happiness was men holding hands as they danced the *dabke*, smiling as they moved towards and away from each other. A woman sang in the center, her voice rising above the drums that kept rhythm with the night. She sang as if she herself had invented magic and for this night alone she was willing to share just a little bit with each of us. A crowd gathered around her, growing larger and rowdier and begging for more. In the hours after midnight men continued to dance, never falling out of step, never slowing down. They only held onto one another's hands more tightly, wanting to hold onto so much more than this night.

By now I knew better than to hold back the tears that swelled in my eyes, so I welcomed them, not only for the first time on this journey, but for one of the first times in my life. When the flood came, it rained down upon me a happiness that I never allowed myself to feel until this moment. Everything else before this was only hindered joy. I brought my hand to my heart, wanting to hold onto this memory and never let it go. I wanted to remember this song, this dance, this night. I wanted to remember this happiness for in those hours I was happy, truly unbelievably deliriously happy. And even though I knew that this happiness was not to last, I also knew now that such happiness exists.

The thing is, we need not cross-continents in search of happiness. For there it may not be found. Like these ferry rides, we go back and forth between one side and the other. But it is never about one side or the another. Most of the time happiness is found in between.

And when my mother calls the next day to ask me how I am, I will tell her that I am happy. Finally, I am happy: wildly, deliciously happy. I did not need to see her to know that she was smiling. I was too. Her wish for me had finally come true. Her daughter was happy. I am happy. And if I close my eyes I am back in Istanbul and I am happy. In Istanbul I was happy.

In the last days of Ramadan, when the month and the moon had no choice but to depart, darkness came crowding the streets with all who have patiently waited to bring food and water to their lips. Celal and I found a table among them. There we ordered too much food and somehow not enough. I blushed, all the while knowing that to eat all of it would be impossible, to not try any of it, a shame. As we ate, Roma came and went between the tables. They danced as they passed speaking to police officers and restaurants owners alike as if they were all part of a performance and it was difficult to tell who the actors were and who was the audience. The youngest and boldest sat next to Celal, her hair fell wildly about her face, her feet barely touched the ground. She flirted from him whatever change he had in his pockets in exchange for a song. Gladly he gave it, singing with her of fallen empires, lost loves, and futures uncertain.

We stayed past midnight, sharing sweet spoonful's of *irmik helvasi* and ordering beer, wine, and even *rakiye*, drunk only on summer and no more. Long after the restaurant closed, we departed, wandering the darkened streets wrapped tightly in one another's arms.

Still awake and not yet ready for sleep we found a bar hidden among the doors of the city. Inside we sat at a table in the corner of the red room lit only by small candles that flickered in the darkness and cast shadows across the walls. Beers, as if there was need for more, were brought to us in tall brown bottles, the amber liquid cold to touch and taste. In the middle of the room a Turkish woman sang; her voice low and steady and strong, as men danced all around her. So similar was this night to the one before that I smiled, remembering the happiness that had been found. As the candles dimmed and the room grew darker, I thought again of time, knowing that even if one hundred years were to pass, this one night in Turkey would be no different now than it was one hundred years before or even one hundred years after. This is the magic of Istanbul. This was the spell that

125

it cast; a spell that has never been broken and will never break.

Since the beginning of this pilgrimage I had been following the path of war, even though war never does follow a path; it bends and breaks everything on either side, destroying whatever path there might have been. And what may have been learned at the end of one war is unlearned at the beginning of the next.

Before I left for Troy, Celal and I spoke of Gallipoli. We spoke of a battle that lasted almost a year, falling silent at the thought of the deaths of 130,842 young men. I told him how little I understood war, how I may never understand it, and how difficult it is to see the glory of war without seeing its wreckage.

Ever the Ottoman, he tsked as the Turkish do and simply said:
"They were trying to destroy our empire. What did you expect?"

Perhaps I expected for history to learn from physics what it cannot seem to learn on its own: that what goes up must also come down.

To cross the Dardanelles, I rode a boat upon gossamer waves towards the sun-drenched hills of the Gallipoli Peninsula. On this small ship men rolled bread in between their fingers and threw it up in the air hoping that the seagulls that followed in our wake would catch these small offerings, but they laughed as each morsel fell, not into the mouths of the birds, but into the sea. I smiled too for it is in these moments I realized that the world, with all its complications, is not always as complicated as we make it to be. Sometimes it is as simple as seagulls and the sea.

In Gallipoli there are monuments that mourn and memorialize the dead. It had been over one hundred years since the battle had taken place, a battle between empires fought by boys. There I did not stay but went in search of a history thousands of years older, wondering all the while how often history needed to repeat itself before it was gotten right.

It should have surprised me, how little is left of Troy: crumbled walls, streets without names, a replication of a horse, this is all that remains. This is for what men fight. Had they known that this what was to become of their follies, would they still have raised their swords? Would they still have given their lives?

Far from the ruins of war I sat under a fig tree. The fruit was not yet ripe but hung bright and green from the branches and I contemplated how long it would be until it would be ready to be plucked. Not one for futures, I thought instead of the past, of my favorite sculpture from antiquity and how here it was never made of stone, but flesh and blood. I imagined how the sea god Poseidon, angered by the thought of the Greeks being less than victorious in this battle sent his serpent to strangle the prophet who had only warned the Trojans of Greeks and their gifts. I imagined the agony with which Laocoön and his sons tried to writhe themselves free. As they drew their last breaths did, they sigh knowing that there will always be those who do not listen; how easily the truths of war fall upon deaf ears.

After, I returned to Istanbul.

Of war, I still knew nothing.

127

Three weeks I stayed in Istanbul. Days passed like lifetimes in which I did everything, and I did nothing. My thoughts were few and they were many. Even now, I cannot think or write of Istanbul without tears in my eyes. So beautiful were my days there that it hurts to think of them as past and not present. Istanbul will always be the city of my heart, the place that made my heart whole. If it was Lebanon that offered me its sweet embrace, then it was Turkey that refused to let me go. Again, I thought of staying forever in Istanbul, but fate propelled me forward; on this journey I was not meant to stand still.

In our last morning together, Celal and I sat down to his table for one last breakfast of hard-boiled eggs, tomatoes, cucumbers, olives, cheese, last night's bread, and cay. The winds were still, and the heat climbed through the open window reminding the two of us how intent summer was to stay and how intent I was to leave.

Not long after, Celal left and I stayed, waiting for my clothes to dry. I sat at his table trying to write him a letter, but it was not Celal who I would miss. It was Istanbul. For it was not Celal who had opened my once hardened heart. It was Istanbul. And so instead I wrote a love letter to the city that had taken my heart into its hands and laid siege to it as it has done for centuries. Here, my heart had been claimed, it had been calmed, it had been conquered.

Dear Istanbul,

Here, in June, orange has become my favorite color: Orange like the rising of your sun in an east so near and the color of your sunset in a west so far. Orange like the color of the thunder moon over the Marmara. Orange like the terra cotta tiles that shelter your city from storms and welcomes sailors in from the tempest. Orange like the flesh of peaches and the skins of apricots. Orange like the ends of cigarettes burning like copper, like rust, like fire in the earliest hours of the morning and the darkest hours of night and all the hours in between. Orange has become my favorite color because it is the color of heat, it is the color of summer, it is the color of you.

Looking back, I wonder if I will remember all of this like a dream where everything is always at its beginnings and nothing, not even summer, comes to an end. I wonder how it is that I could leave a place in which happiness did not exist for me until here.

Because of this I will always remember my first coffee in Istanbul. I will remember the ceramic cup in which it was served with blues more blue than the Bosphorus laced with red and white and a handle so delicate that I had to lift it up from its rim in fear of shattering its beauty. I will remember the flakes of coconut that fell from that first Turkish Delight onto the saucer that matched this cup and the sweetness that it contained. If I close my eyes, I can still taste this coffee on my tongue: strong and bitter and almost as hot as the sun that shone without clouds in the sky. I can still hear the call to prayer echo from Asia to Europe and back again. I will remember how still I stood, listening to this prayer and having to remind myself to breathe for in these moments my very breath had been taken from me, every other emotion but happiness had been taken from me and I wanted none of them back. But this happiness I would like to keep, for you are my happiness, you are my home.

Teşekkürler Stamboul

129

Seni seviyorum. Seni her zaman seveceğim. Always.

Me

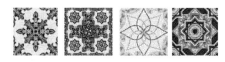

     After my clothes were dry and my bags were packed, I returned to Sultanahmet to stand with Celal until it was time to leave, knowing already that I was never to see him again. And then came one last sunset, one last call to prayer, setting the sky on fire and so, too, my heart. I gazed across the Marmara, knowing both the beauty of one side and of the other and all the beauty in between. I closed my eyes wanting to remember only this:

The space between need not always be filled. Empty, it can echo our hopes and dreams and call us back to all the places we call home.

From the Sea
To the Mountains

I cried as I boarded the bus and watched the city of Istanbul fade into the night. Gone were the turrets of The Blue Mosque, gone were the boats and ferries of the Bosphorus, and gone were the days and nights spent walking from east to west only to return east once more. But it was time. My heart longed for all the things that cannot be found in a city. For me, Istanbul had grown too crowded, too full and I needed to be reminded of things that have always been and will always be bigger than me.

On the night train from Istanbul, I was lucky enough to have a whole compartment to myself; another simple pleasure never to be taken for granted and always to be grateful for. As the train gathered speed and moved further away from the city, I knew that I was not soon to come back. Day broke somewhere between Turkey and Bulgaria and we arrived in Sofia under a cloudless sky and an ever-unconquerable sun. Again, there would be no rain.

Once off the train, I met a young Dutchman who had also just been in Istanbul. He laughed when he

134

learned that I had come to Bulgaria to hug some trees. Little did he know that this was not just a flippant desire to be among wild things, but a deep-rooted ache to seek all that was wild inside of me. More than anything I missed the woods. I missed trees and the heights they go to for just a little light. I missed the way that the wind whispers stories if we stay quiet enough to listen and I missed who I was when there was no need to be tame.

After Turkey everything seemed so uncrowded and unencumbered. The broad boulevards of Sofia spread from the station, making the city seem that over the course of its construction it had grown wide more than it had grown tall where Soviet architecture stood side by side with the excavated ruins of bygone eras. So early in the morning we checked into the hostel and then returned to explore the city.

Sofia can trace its roots back almost seven thousand years, rooting itself in the Paleolithic era before falling under the influence of both the Thracian and Roman Empires. Over the course of centuries, the city changed hands so often that it came to be known only as the place between mountains. In 1382, the city of Sofia fell to the Turks, marking the beginning of five hundred years of Ottoman rule. It finally found its independence in 1844, an independence that lasted only one hundred years before it fell again, this time behind the Iron Curtain. We spent almost the entire day moving in and out of Byzantine churches, their walls covered in frescoes, their ceilings domed vaults. For lunch and for dinner we ate Balkan pastries and borek and for the first time in months the influence of the West was more apparent than that of the East.

In the distance rose Cherni Vrah, the Black Peak of Vitosha Mountain, calling me from its heights beyond the city. Much of this journey had been spent at the level of the sea, sometimes even below, but tomorrow this

135

mountain was to be climbed. Only once before had I climbed a mountain, on another continent, at another time.

Late in the afternoon clouds rolled into the valley, holding in their grasp promises of rain. But these promises were not to be kept and the clouds parted revealing the summer sun.

In the morning a cab was taken to the foot of the mountain, the top hidden from view, the path winding through a forest of ancient trees: white pines, planes and oaks whose shadows danced with the sun. For most of the way the trail was well marked. After all, up is up. No longer on flat ground, those first steps were the most challenging. My heart pounded. My lungs ached. Not conditioned for such a physical exertion, I wanted to turn around and go back down. More than once I stopped after just ten steps for my lungs and my heart would not and could not empty or fill fast enough. It was torture, and yet somehow bliss. With each step it seemed as if the mountain said to me: "You are almost there," even though it was not even close. That mountain was a liar, but man, were those sweet little lies.

When there was no further to go, the wind swept over the mountain and wildflowers rocked in its rush. There was not a soul was to be seen; how strange it was to go from being in a city of millions to alone at the top of the world. And while this top might have only measured some seven thousand feet, it was high enough for me.

Before leaving on this pilgrimage, my dear friend Lisa gave me a picture of her daughter, Courtney, who she had lost just two years ago in a car accident and asked me to take her with me on this journey. And so, she came with me in the form of a photograph and in my heart, I carried memories of Melissa, my best friend who lost her battle with cancer when we were just nine years old. For

136

almost thirty years Melissa had stayed by my side and here was no different. For I had learned a long time ago that there is no sense in going anywhere without angels. How else are they to get their wings?

Climbing Vitosha was an exercise in humility and with each step I learned that I may slip, but I will not fall. I may soften, but I will not weaken. I may slow, but I will not stop, and I began to realize that I am still learning something of patience although it is not a quality that I freely possess. I am still learning of the patience that is required for the climbing of mountains. I am learning to have patience with my feet for not moving faster, and then, how fast slow becomes in the contemplation of time. I am learning, patiently, just how beautiful it is to wait for the wind. It is patience like the coming of rain, the lifting of mist, the rising of the sun.

I stayed at the top of Vitosha until a chill pierced the summer air and came down the only way to come down from a mountain: triumphant, returning to Sofia only until morning, until the first and last bus to Rila departed.

In Rila there is a monastery that is nestled between mountains. Its roofs are red, and its walls are painted green and white with thick beams of wood coursing through each story, mirroring the forest that it is surrounded by and sometimes even the sky. In the tenth century, the students of the hermit St. Ivan of Rila, the patron saint of Bulgarians, built the complex in reverence for their teacher. In 1833 it burnt to the ground and was rebuilt into the grandeur it is today. In the gloaming the doors were closed to all visitors except for those who were to spend the night and as the sun tucked itself under a blanket of clouds the vespers could be heard, lulling me to an early slumber filled with dreams of mountains just within reach.

137

As first light crept in from the east, I slipped out of my chambers to watch the monks gather in the chapel, shuffling in from their sleep in their black cassocks, their beards long and their heads covered with kalimavkion. The sun rose over the mountains, each ray of light piercing through the trees, illuminating the valley below. In the quickening day pigeons dipped and swooped in the courtyard; the colors of their feathers changing in the changing light, purple on the way up and golden as they came down.

After coffee I set out along the river to climb another mountain even though I had no idea where I was going; I was only hoping for up. Even with maps, the trails were not well marked, but stubborn that I am, I continued to climb until the 'trail' ended abruptly on the edge of a cliff; a waterfall to the left and to the right, a valley full of trees every color green; summer at its fullest, nature at its most sublime. The wind rushed like a river through this valley, rustling the leaves all at once. Nothing was silent. Nothing was still. And I stood small among mountains knowing less, understanding less, needing less.

After this, I never wanted to return to cities.

After this, forever I wanted to stay in the mountains.

Long before dawn I boarded a bus to Serbia. It was a quiet ride, save for the two men in the seats in front of me who were more awake than the rest of us at so early an hour. When we stopped for rest after the border, one of them spoke to me, first in Russian, then in Serb-Croat, and finally in English; commanding use of them all. I answered him only in English and while it surprised him to find an American so far away from home, it pleased him to practice one of the five languages he speaks. For what remained of the bus ride he told the abbreviated history of the former Yugoslavia, most of which I never knew for growing up in the United States at the end of the Cold War I was taught little more than to fear and vilify what lay behind the Iron Curtain.

Again, over the course of this conversation, I was reminded that history is not one-dimensional; its sides are many, its angles obtuse and acute and never transparent; sometimes only side can be seen and not the other. Through every country traveled, this was the story that was told: there is no desire for war, revolution perhaps, but most want only the opportunity to live their lives fully and quietly, a home in which to raise their

139

children and return to at the end of a long day, and peace however it can be found.

Arriving in Nis there was no sun; the air was cool and felt not of summer. Clouds gathered like a conquering army around the city and finally it rained. For this I had been waiting for eighty-six days. But this rain did not to last; it was fleeting, falling ever so briefly in the afternoon and by morning, the clouds had all but disappeared and the sun returned to shine down upon Serbia.

In 272 AD a boy was born in Naissus, Moesia, now the Serbian city of Nis. He was the son of a Roman army officer and a Greek mother who rose through the ranks of the Roman guard to eventually become the emperor of Rome. His Latin name was Constantine, the man who proclaimed Christianity to be the true religion of the empire and the man who moved its capital to his namesake: Constantinople.

To Nis I went to witness the cruelty of history; a history written by the victors that warns of the consequences of rebellion and resistance. Here, there is a tower that stands on the outskirts of the city. It is constructed entirely from human skulls; all that remain of the men who fought against the Ottomans in the First Serbian Uprising in 1809. Around and around the tower I walked counting how many people were willing to lose their lives for freedom rather than spend the rest of their lives in a cage.

From Nis, I boarded a bus to Belgrade. Since 441 BCE, Belgrade has been destroyed and rebuilt, conquered and retaken more than forty times. Fearing the irrational fear that history may repeat itself while I was there, I stayed in the city just long enough to spend the night and then took the first bus back into the mountains, this time to Tara, so named after the Slavic God Tar. In Tara I was tempted again by thoughts of

140

stillness but did not stay. Soon, my pockets would be empty, all the money that I had worked so hard to save, and I wanted to at least get to Spain before that happened.

The next morning the bus stop was only four kilometers away and so I set off down the road with my bag on my back, knowing the distance was more near than far. Barely did I make it a kilometer before a woman stopped and offered me a ride in her van. Of course, I said yes and as luck would have it, she was passing through Bosnia on her way further east to Montenegro. As she steered the van back onto the road, she apologized in her perfect English for it being flawed and asked me to correct her if she were to make a mistake. But I was in no position to do so, for so poetic was her command of a language that she spoke as her second that to find fault in it would be to insult.

Her name was Lubitza and for most of the journey she leaned her head against her hand, the window open, and the winds of summer passing through her copper hair. She had the habit of moving her bottom jaw from side to side while she thought as if turning the words she was about to speak over on her tongue wondering if they would sound as they tasted. Over borders we talked about the complication of politics and with nonchalance, she spoke of the probability of an autumn revolution. She admitted:
"I think September there will be a rebellion. The people are not happy, but now it is summer, and everyone is on holiday, so September it will happen." She said this with the casualness of a woman who knew about war, perhaps more than she knew about peace.

As we continued to speak about history, she held onto the wheel the way she still holds onto Tito: tightly and loosely, with reverence and with fear. She spoke of the former president of the former Yugoslavia as one

141

speaks of their favorite uncle. She missed him in the same way too, as if a part of her died in May of 1980 and nothing has ever been the same. Maybe sometimes it is easier to hold onto an unrepeatable past than an uncertain present.

Nearer to Bosnia, Lubitza began to recall the seventy-eight days of Operation Allied Force in 1999, when the North Atlantic Treaty Organization bombed Yugoslavia during the Kosovo War. For a moment the van was silent as if we both were trying to determine just how many wrongs make a right. But war never differentiates between the two, war knows not the difference.

For her kindness I took her to lunch of *cevapi*, a meal of meat and bread, at a restaurant with a view of the bridge of Visegrad, made famous by both war and poetry. After we walked across the bridge, standing in the middle just long enough for her to translate the poem inscribed on the center stone and then she left.

As she drove away, I thought to myself that we enter and leave people's lives in the most haphazard ways: arriving unexpectedly and sometimes departing the same way. And that maybe this world, full of its complications and all its pleasures, would not seem so daunting if we knew just how much of this journey we share.

From Visegrad I took a bus to Sarajevo; a place I almost did not go because it took me further south and west of Poland, where I wanted to begin my walk in earnest, but I was so often told that if I were to write of war, then Sarajevo was not to be missed.

The Siege of Sarajevo lasted for three years, ten months, and twenty-four days; three times longer than that of Stalingrad and a year more than Leningrad. Over the course of the Bosnian War, one hundred thousand people were killed, including eight thousand men and boys massacred in Srebrenica with thousands more were displaced both within and beyond the borders of Bosnia. The most vicious among the perpetrators referred to the Bosnian War as revenge against the Muslims for Ottoman rule. The strongest of the survivors called it what it was, what war is: a tragedy, a genocide, a cruel history, and an even crueler fate.

In the morning there was a walking tour through the streets of Sarajevo. In one of the squares of the city I joined the large crowd waiting for our guide to arrive, which she did and gathered us close before we began. She was fair of skin with dark hair that was pulled back in a thick ponytail that covered the nape of her neck and revealed eyes that had seen more violence in four years than most see their entire lives. Her and I were born in the same year, but months and worlds apart.

143

It is not always the stars that reveal our fate. More often than not it is the ground below our feet that determines our destiny.

A canal runs through the center of the city, the water is shallow but steady as it carves its way around small rocks that did little to impede its flow. Surrounding Sarajevo mountains rise, both protecting and entrapping those that live in the narrow valley below. In the shade we stopped to learn of a past that is ever so present on the streets of Sarajevo. Like Lebanon, there are small holes carved by bullets in nearly every building of the old town. I imagined that if you put your ear close enough to the punctured walls, you could still hear the ricochet of the copper and lead that clashed and crashed against the brick and mortar.

Somewhere in the middle of our tour we passed the place where the Archduke Franz Ferdinand was assassinated. Our guide told us that for many years following the war these five Young Serbs, on whose shoulders often rests the responsibility of beginning the First World War, were regarded as heroes. But years later, after the fall of communism they were vilified as bringing about the destruction of the world as it was then known.

War does this: revering in one moment what is reviled in the next.

As we continued to walk through history, our guide, who had been a child during the Bosnian-Serbian War, spoke of all the games that she and her friends use to play in those years; whether they were played to stay sane or to embrace the insanity, it was difficult to tell. She told of one game that was played every day on her way home from school, when there was still a school for them to go. In the afternoons she and her friends, running as

144

fast as they could to their houses, would compete to find the largest shrapnel or bullet that rained down upon them from the snipers that lay in wait in the hills surrounding the city. When they arrived safely inside their courtyards, they compared what had been found, opening their palms to reveal their haul. In some sort of dystopian Goldilocks parable of war, they said to one another:

"Mine is too small."

"Mine is too big."

Until finally the last of them confessed:

"Mine is still hot."

And with that the game was won.

As the summer grew in length, so did the heat and our guide lead us to a fountain, one of the many of the city. Here we refilled our water bottles from the cool clean taps. She paused, inhaling deeply before beginning another story. Listening intently, I could not tell what was more difficult for her: to return to the past or come back from it. When she had collected herself, she told us of how the United Nations would deliver food during the siege, but never water. She went on to say that when the U.N. troops were present the snipers that hid in the hills would not train their guns on what was below and she never understood that if that was the case, then why did the peace keeping troops not stay? Perhaps, had they stayed, eight thousand Bosniak men would not have disappeared into unmarked graves. Perhaps, had they stayed; the war would not have lasted so long. Perhaps, had they stayed; they would have brought with them peace they were meant to keep. She ended our tour by counting the days of the war once more. Three years. Ten months. Twenty-four days. Three years. Ten months. Twenty-four days. Long enough for children to be born and for men to die; long enough for so many terrible and beautiful things to happen.

145

Perhaps it is only the ticking of time that keeps the past in its place; each second creating more distance between then and now, war and peace.

From Sarajevo a small bus was taken again into the mountains. On these often-pleasurable sojourns whole families sat next to one another in small seats crammed with bags and suitcases, leaving just enough room for crossed arms and legs. Always once, in the middle of our journey, a stop was made for coffee so that we may stretch our legs, smoke cigarettes, and exchange smiles. There we would stay for almost an hour before setting off down the road again.

Switchback by switchback we wound up the narrow pass before entering the valley of Sutjeska National Park, the mountains rising on either side as if in perpetual competition with the sky. The rural road was marked by a hotel less grand than it once was, scattered shacks and houses, and the Tjentiste War Memorial, an abstract monument that was erected in 1970 to commemorate the Yugoslavian forces that thwarted a Nazi advance through this valley in the Second World War.

My hotel had been missed by two kilometers and I walked back down the hill to find it. It was run by a man who had only just returned to Bosnia after twenty-five years in exile. He came back to begin life again in the mountains. I was almost silly enough to ask him why it was that he had been gone for so long but stopped just before the words escaped my mouth. In hesitant English he showed me where I was to stay: a small room with small windows, surrounded by mountains. There was nowhere else in the world that I would rather be. It was summer, it was quiet, and it was perfect.

When darkness descended into the valley I stood underneath a veil of clouds, waiting for stars. First came Venus, the goddess of love and victory and chosen guardian for this journey. She rose over the eastern hills and for the shortest of moments she stood alone in the sky. For the first time in months the air was cool and the whole of my body had forgotten what the world felt like without heat. Under the filament I stayed with a blanket wrapped tightly around me, imagining this to be the place where stars came when they fell, to finally rest and fall no more.

The sun rose over the rocky peaks, casting its warmth and light across the valley. I dressed for breakfast and crossed the street to Makadam restaurant. Here in this place mostly of men I was an anomaly: a lone American woman intent on mountains. I ordered a coffee and although it is almost the same as Turkish coffee, here they call it *domaca*, brewed strong, dark and thick and served in a larger cup, as if still attempting to shake off the dust of five hundred years of Ottoman rule. A plate arrived filled with hard-boiled eggs, cured meats, jam and a basket of bread; the breakfast of the Balkans. The meal like the morning moved slowly. There was no rush.

From Bosnia, I was trying to get to Poland to begin my Camino on the Lesser Polish Way, but it seemed for that, there was no longer a need. For I soon discovered that Poland had come to me in the form of two Polish gentlemen riding their motorbikes on holiday through the Balkans. Their names were Christopher and Magic. Both hovered around their forties, balancing one another on either side. Christopher was the father of two who lived in the Netherlands and Magic had recently

147

moved from the town that he loved in the mountains of Poland to Birmingham, England for opportunities that he was no longer convinced existed. Magic had salt and pepper hair with eyes that spoke of both skies and oceans. Only the day before Magic had had an accident; falling off his motorbike somewhere between one turn and another and he was now in need of rest and recovery. Flirt that I am I asked him to join me for a small hike in the hills. Flirt that he is, he said yes.

After breakfast we made our way to the trailhead, walking in steady steps up the sloping hill. Every now and again we took sips from a bottle of hooch that we had brought with us for the climb; each sip of Rakia sweet and harsh on my tongue. As we walked, we talked about all the things that I like to talk about best: life and love, people and the past. He told the history of his country that I never knew despite my grandmother having lived in Poland until just weeks before September 1, 1939. He told these stories as if this history had already been forgotten, or worse, that history had been erased and needed to be written again and remembered. He was proud to be Polish, proud to be born among people who believed in their land and their lives even when it seemed that the rest of the world did not.

Halfway up the hill the weather grew warmer as bits of sunlight pierced through the trees. Magic stopped at one of the fountains on the side of the hill to pull the shirt from his back, his sweat dripping down the length of his spine. Twice he filled his bottle with water: the first he poured over his shirtless skin and the second he guzzled as if only now was he learning what it means to thirst. I pretended to look away. I was here to climb a mountain and no more.

Eventually the incline leveled off and the mountains spread before us, rising in waves of limestone and granite. In the distance, almost hidden from view

148

was a waterfall, seemingly coming out of nowhere and disappearing all the same. Together we stood in silence, mesmerized by the water as it fell. We welcomed this quiet, each in our own rapturous reverie of this perfect summer day. On our way back down he turned to me, breaking the silence to ask:
"What do you love about America?"
Without missing a beat, I responded:
"Pizza."

Which, if you ask me, is as good of an answer as any, but then again, pizza was not necessarily American, but a tradition of New York (and sometimes Chicago) so I suppose my love for America is partial, it is almost impossible for me to love it whole. Apparently, pizza was not the answer that he was looking for because, he rationalized, pizza could be gotten anywhere. Poor guy, he had never had a slice from New York before. And yet further he pressed, trying to understand a country that to him was incomprehensible.
"Seriously, I would like to know. What do you love about America?"

It was a difficult question. I had left America unable to understand it, heartbroken that in the twenty-first century, we found ourselves no further socially, politically, or culturally than the century before. How do you explain to someone who is not American, what the American dream is while still convincing yourself that such a dream exists? And so I paused, searching for the words that had been lost, like so many other things, in the election of last year.
"What I love about America is not necessarily America as it is, but what it can be." He slowed his steps and I took his silence as an opportunity to ask him the same. He smiled mischievously and responded with a single word: Kielbasa.

On our way down he confessed that despite living in England this was the most English that he had ever spoken. I laughed and told him that it was the same for me. That night, we ate dinner together, filled with food, beer, and more Rakia than I remember. Sometime after midnight, Magic walked me to my room and we said our goodbyes, he to his bed and me to mine. Some men are not to be known.

In the morning another attempt was made for Maglic, the mountain that stands the tallest of the Dinaric Alps. The intention was to hitchhike to the footpath that leads to the top, but still a stranger to mountains I got too late a start and I knew before I even set off that the top was not to be reached. And still I climbed, retracing the steps taken only the day before.

An hour passed without cars or people, the quiet solitude of the morning giving way to an ever more silent afternoon. Within the second hour I considered giving up because there might not be enough time to summit the mountain and return before dark. But then a car was heard, crunching the gravel under its tires as it made the slow climb up the road. Sticking my thumb out into the air, the driver stopped, and I climbed into the passenger seat of the old pick-up truck with a father and his son. The man spoke no English and I no Croat, but we were moving in the same direction and he was kind enough to stop and let me in. Besides who needs language when so much can be understood without it? His fingernails were stained with oil, as were his overalls. He wore an old baseball cap, the cotton kind with a metal clasp in the back, which was also smudged, the grease spreading from the rim to the button, turning the hat from blue to brown. There were wrenches and plastic funnels about the cab. A traveling mechanic perhaps, or simply a man who has spent much of his life traversing this mountain and knows that it is better to be prepared than stranded.

The road was unpaved, and we bounced over rocks and pebbles. While in low gear he handed his young child a large bottle of beer, which the boy opened with the dexterity of someone who had done this on more than one occasion and now considered himself a professional. He handed it back to his father, who then offered me a sip, then one to his son, before taking his own. Although I said no, they continued to pass the bottle back and forth, taking silent sips and keeping their eyes on the road. When he pulled his car to the side of the road, I spoke the only phrase I knew in Croat, which is often the only phrase ever needed while traveling: *Hvala vam.* Thank you. He pointed me in the direction of the path that led to Maglic. Collecting my bags and thanking him again, I walked off wondering just how safe I was out here all by myself with what little expertise I had in climbing mountains. This was not the smartest thing that I ever did on this journey and once again I found myself high on a hill without a single soul in sight and, aside from my new friend and his son, no one else knew where I was.

Walking deeper into the primordial forest, the trees rose on either side shutting out the sunlight and stilling the air. Letting my imagination get the best of me, I began to imagine this place to be the Fire Swamp from the Princess Bride and with every step I stayed on high alert for rodents of unusual size, or as they like to call them in Bosnia: bears. Looking right and then left and then right again, I picked up a stick only half of my height, more frail than it was sturdy, as if this alone would deter any animal who stood in my way. I think my heart, even after all those years of playing sports, had never beaten so fast.

151

The road bent and twisted, sloping down only to angle back up. Around a curve the way opened and all that could be seen was mountain after mountain. They spread so far and so wide that it was difficult to imagine what lay beyond these hills. I sat on the edge of the world looking out into the distance, the silence deafening, the peace profound, surrendering to the thought that mountains do not stand in defiance of the flat earth, they stand as testament to what is possible if only we allow ourselves to shift. A noise broke the quiet hush, somewhere between a huff and a growl, far enough away to be mistaken, but close enough not to be ignored. It might have only been for the howl of the wind but alone, halfway up a mountain and only halfway through my journey this was not the way I wanted to go out. But then again, if I were to die in the arms of a bear, this view alone would have been worth it. Knowing that most of the time it is better to be safe than it is to be stupid, I came down from the mountain never having seen the top but still promising to return to Maglic one day.

The day came for me to leave Sutjeska, but now to Italy instead of Poland. Perhaps I had temporarily lost the plot, but geographically Italy was closer than Poland- and easier to get to- and it was still on my way west to Spain.

By the Balkans I had come to rely on my extremities: my feet for walking, my ears for listening, my hands for breaking bread, but it was my thumbs that had been put to the best use for there is no better way to get from one place to another, one country to another than hitchhiking. Now I can count on both of my thumbs the number of times I have hitchhiked before; the first was in college and the last some years later when a tire on my pickup truck refused to stay whole. Otherwise it is in the driver's seat that I have always found myself holding on tightly, too tightly, to the wheel. It has only been on the rarest of occasions that I have allowed myself to let go. And yet in Bosnia, in the middle of July, in the middle of these mountains, I finally learned to do just that and I departed Bosnia in the same way as I arrived: as a unexpected passenger in the car of a women who refused to leave another woman stranded on the side of the road.

Adina was ever so like Lubitza, the woman who brought me into Bosnia, except for one stark contrast: whereas Lubitza is an Orthodox Serbian, Adina is a Bosnian Muslim. Other than this, their differences were few. They were about the same age; one had only just entered her sixth decade and the other was soon to leave it. Like me, life had rendered them single and they both traveled alone to the mountains of Montenegro and the coast of Croatia. I had the sense that as the years continue to pass as they have in my life I could easily be either one of these women and, with hope, I might one day be able to pay their kindness forward along this road called life.

In her English, which Adina spoke with the quiet confidence of a woman who learned this language not first, but second, she asked if I was scared to be traveling alone to which I always answer no. For I am more afraid of not traveling than I am of traveling alone; solitude is a blessing, a stationary life, a curse.

Our conversation came with ease, escaping from and returning to the past as the miles and the mountains unfolded before us. With kilometers came comfort except that we did not speak of those three years and eight months of war between Serbia and Bosnia, only the

153

years before and the years after. She was happy to have me in her company as we passed through Trebijne, fearful to be alone when driving through a town known for its violence and its extremes. As we drew closer to Croatia, Adina told how she fled the country of her heart in 1992 and sought refuge in Germany. She has been there for twenty-five years. She has been there ever since. With reverence she, too, spoke of Tito and how her experiences with communism were better than her experiences without. So much so that I began to believe that, given the opportunity, she would also go back to the way things were before the death of Tito, before the wall fell, and before the wars began.

Closing in on our destination I began to count all of my blessings on all of my extremities for being able to share this journey not only with Adina now, but with Lubitza before as well, to be able to share in their histories and in their presence for despite how congested this world might sometimes seem, most of us are indeed traveling in the same direction and if we are willing to release the reigns every once in a while there are so many humans out there who are willing, more than willing to help us get to all of the places that we wish to go and, if we are lucky, some may take us further than we ever imagined; they might just carry us over mountains, they just might lead us to the sea.

As Adina's car drew once again to the side of the road, this time to let me out rather than let me in, I thought that maybe this lonely lonely world would not seem so lonely if only we stopped and picked each other up every once in a while.

Sometimes it is the best way; sometimes it is the only way, to get from one place to another.

AN ODYSSEY

Once in Croatia, there was a night in Dubrovnik and no more. At noon the ferry set sail across the Aegean. There was no real reason to go to Italy. It was never part of my journey, but maybe it is that fate was being funny and, after leaving the shores of Ilium, the winds led me to lands west on an odyssey all my own. I thought maybe Florence was a good idea and then thought better of it. There I was not meant to stay either. To pass the time in the heart of the Renaissance, an entire day was spent at a restaurant speaking on the phone with my best friend, my RHB while eating gnocchi and drinking enough wine for the two of us to share even though she was in America and I was in Italy. As the heat thought it in its best interest to rise, I thought it in my best interest to stay where I was and move on to Aperol Spritzers. For the rest of that furnace of an afternoon I watched the ice melt; making the bittersweet liquid clearer and my mind just the opposite. I was a cliché of the worst and best kind, not that it mattered; so hot was the day, so unbearable the heat, what else was I to do?

That night, surprisingly still able to stand, I stumbled back to the hostel, and slept the sleep of the restless. I left Florence just as soon as I arrived for I am not made for the cities. I do not like to put bars around my heart.

Call it romantic, call it ridiculous, call it what you will, but I always like to make my escape in the middle of the night. And so it was at midnight that I began my journey of seventeen hours north and then west to France, staying in Milan just long enough to sleep for two hours on the floor of the bus station, but not long enough to see the Duomo and before dawn I crossed the border. I had gone to France with the hope of finally finding a quiet place where my pen can easily find the page and I could begin to put words to this journey.

But hope is a funny thing; how it fools you into believing all the things that even your heart knows not to be true.

Oft impulsive, especially when it comes to decisions that require more thought, I do not always think things through and this decision was definitely the dumbest that was made on this pilgrimage: to house sit in the middle of nowhere for a Dutchman with three large dogs who had once been a peace keeping officer for the United Nations. I stayed for one night and was gone by morning. I had not even unpacked my bags. Without surprise, he dropped me off in the town below and I hitched a ride with a truck driver to the train station. By nightfall I was in Aix-en-Provence to see about an old friend, long gone but somehow still with me.

Morning came, the sun lackadaisically rising over the south of France; a little softer, a little later. The leaves had begun to brown, and autumn did as autumn

159

does so late in the summer, it eased itself into August caring not that its time had not yet come.

Just after ten I walked through the small gate that marked the entrance of the Atelier of Paul Cezanne. I cried as I entered. This was the house where he painted portraits, where he painted fruit, where he painted mountains. Tubes of paint, squeezed and sold, lay where the artist left them, among his brushes and rags. A single glass of wine, empty yet stained crimson stood next to a bowl of fruit; a final still life, a reminder that not all is meant to last. Easels leaned in the corners next to overcoats and topcoats that still hung from hooks on the wall. Three skulls, browned by the years sat atop a marble shelf, with three pairs of eyes staring into the distance. By the open window I sat on a wooden bench, his wooden bench, listening to the cars pass below, wondering what it might have been like to have heard a car pass, a telephone ring, or the sound of a steam engine for the first time; what it might have been like to see the nineteenth century end and the twentieth begin. I wondered what it might have been like to know such an artist.

When the day folded itself in half I returned to the hostel on top of the hill. It was house run by a handsome Frenchman. He had grown up within these walls and even though his family lived no longer lived there he wished not to part with it. In the darkness that fell before eight and not after, we spoke of many things. Not wanting our conversation to end we made plans for the next day.

In the soft light of an August morning we met in the cobblestoned square where we gathered what was needed for an afternoon picnic. After sharing a cup of coffee, we rode with no plans except to explore the hills of Provence. Without rush, we pedaled away from the city, the sun warm, the wind soft, and my heart quiet. For

160

lunch we shared a baguette filled with cured ham and local cheese. For dessert there was a single chocolate chip cookie. To him, it was the best cookie in the world, and maybe for that day it was.

After, Gregoire slept and I swam naked in a pool of piercing blue water sheltered by limestone rocks worn and white from the sun, asking again for those old wounds to be healed. It was the ninth of August. It was the twenty-eighth August without Melissa. Ripples ran across the surface of the water, spreading in concentric waves across the reservoir and I knew then that she was with me. I remembered the ripples she created every time she dove into a pool. I remembered the ripples she created everywhere she went. And I knew that every day that the sun shone on this journey that she had been with me. She had been with me from the beginning just as she would be with me to the very end.

The sun arced west, waking Gregoire from his sieste and together we sat side by side, our bronzed bare skin touching and our feet dangling in the turquoise water. We were joined at the joints: knees, shoulders, and hips and even though it would have been easier to get closer, we did not. We stayed this way until goose bumps rose to the tops of our thighs and the backs of our arms. It was the first time in my life that I experienced such intimacy with a man without need for anything more. When voices were heard across the quarry we dressed, our skin still wet, and rode our bicycles to the foot of Mont Sainte-Victoire. Soon there would be darkness. In the fading light that confused blue for gray we hiked to the top of the mountain, scrambling up the stone path that carved its way up the pass. Climbing ever higher I knew why Cezanne returned here until the very last day of his life. Here was earth. Here was heaven.

We stayed until the sun grew as big as the sky. Gregoire pointed east to the Alps. The mountains were

161

calling him too. As we descended, I turned my head towards Mont Sainte Victoire, afraid to take my eyes off her, as if, after all these years she might disappear. With each turn the colors shifted from coral to magenta and as the sun said its final goodbye to the day the mountain was as pink as the sky.

As night fell on Provence we rode back to Aix, coasting down the hills, the taillights of our bikes flickering in the darkness. On the edge of the city we parted with a kiss on the cheek and a swift embrace. Just before midnight I boarded another bus to Bordeaux, arriving at first light with just enough time for coffee and a croissant before continuing to Spain, where I was to begin my journey on foot across its north coast. In front of the cathedral there was a market and rather than buying anything, I left on a table a pair of pants bought in India, the scarf that kept me warm and safe throughout this journey, and THE dress, the perfect pink dress complete with pockets full of memories that Celal had bought me in Istanbul. Parting with this dress was the one and only regret that I had on this journey.

But now was no time for nostalgia. Now was the time for letting go.

A WALK IN THE RAIN

There is no coming to consciousness without pain. People will do anything, no matter how absurd, in order to avoid facing their own soul. One does not become enlightened by imagining figures of light, but by making the darkness conscious.
~ Carl Jung.

The histories of the Camino are many and their roots are tangled with paganism, Christianity, and even Islam. Pagans who inhabited the Iberian Peninsula made pilgrimages on the *Via Lactae*, or the Milky Way; a path on earth said to mirror the heavens. The Romans called the place where the path meets to the sea, *Finis Terrea*, "the end of the world." The legend of Saint James begins in the first century when Santiago traveled to this remote corner of Roman Hispania to spread the gospel. Upon his return to Palestine, James was tortured and beheaded by Herodes Agrippa, otherwise known as Herod, King of Judea. Forbidden burial, his disciples spirited his body back to Spain where they buried the Apostle in a field of stars, *Campus Stellae*, what is now known as Santiago de Compostela. When his tomb was rediscovered in the ninth century, a chapel was built in its place and

Christians from across the Holy Roman Empire began flocking to the site of his final resting place to revere the saint.

For the centuries that followed the Camino has been traveled by pilgrims in search of holiness, in search of wisdom, and in search of salvation and I, in search of something, was no different.

On the train to Irun I remembered conversations that were had with Muslims in Lebanon, Jordan and Palestine in which I was often told that the true jihad is not the one being waged against the world, it is the jihad that is waged against our greatest adversary, our own worst enemy, our darkest night. Muslims call this *jihad al-nafs*: the jihad of the soul.

So much of this journey was an attempt to understand wars of the past and the present but four months on I had barely faced my own darkness and it was my hope that on the Camino, that the very shadows where I hid my fears, faults, mistakes and regrets, would be brought to light.

For I have always believe that wars will always be waged if we do not first fight the battle within.

Forever in motion, my feet, like my heart, do not know how to stand still. Which is why, in my reckless youth I sought everything that moves: sports, the sun, and the sea. And now, with the years passing with the same suddenness and speed that was reveled when time was taken for granted and rebelled against now that it is known that nothing can be done to stop this time from going on, I still seek the same. This is also why, even as I drag thirty behind me kicking and screaming to meet its fate of forty, I am unwilling to give up my youth, just as I am unwilling to give up my love for the sea, that I found myself in the northeast corner of Spain in the beginning of August ready for the real adventure to begin.

Walking the Camino de Santiago was always the 'final' intention of this journey; I just began a little further east than most. But I chose to walk El Camino de Norte, a solitary track along the north coast of Spain instead of the heavily trafficked Via Frances because after four months of traveling through city after city, country after country, and walking among millions of people, I was in need of quietude, for I am solitary, I am stubborn, and I am competitive. Socially, these are not the most endearing qualities but when it comes to crossing almost an entire country on foot there is no other way I would rather be.

On Thursday the tenth of August, I arrived in Irun, a small seaside city in Spain that often serves as the starting point for many pilgrims on the Northern Way. With ease the *albergue*, a small hostel meant to house pilgrims along the Camino, was found. Once through the open doors the *hospitalero*, a volunteer who cares for pilgrims, welcomed me inside and stamped my Credencials del Peregrino for the very first time. Other peregrinos, pilgrims who had also chosen the El Camino del Norte, were already there. In their hands they held guides, actual paperback books with dog-eared pages marked with post-its charting the journey ahead. But my hands were empty, and soon, so would be my pockets. Only $500 remained of the thousands of dollars that I had saved for this trip and I had already decided that I would walk until I had not a penny to my name. Money and maps be damned.

That night, in the small kitchen of the albergue, a simple meal was made of stewed tomatoes and peppers over a bed of rice and shared with other pilgrims Although we were of various ages and backgrounds all of us were excited to begin our pilgrimages the next day even though none of us knew how far it might take us, or how deep.

That first morning I woke before my alarm. The sun had not risen and would not rise for hours, but after a sleepless, but not soundless night, I dressed by the light of a flashlight, hoping not to forget anything but the extra and unnecessary weight that was to be left behind. I rolled up my sleeping bag, laced my boots, and set out into the darkness. Ahead the day was long and said to be difficult.

Within the first hour I got lost. It was not my fault. Had the sunrise not been so beautiful I might not have chased it, forgetting that I am walking west and not east, but there was the sun stealing shadows from the night and giving the day its dawn. When the path was found again, it went up into the mountains along dirt and rock switchbacks. Both sides of the trail were lined with Eucalyptus and Pine trees, offering shade when it was needed and light when it was not. Cool air spread from under the canopy of trees and the heat, so sharp for so long softened as summer shortened.

As the way sloped and fell, I came upon an old man out on his morning walk. He wore a tan flat cap with matching pants and jacket. He climbed the hill with ease, his steps falling in rhythm with his walking stick that scraped the rocky ground. As he passed, he traced a *flecha*,

169

a small yellow arrow found at almost every turn on the Camino, with the end of his stick. He said there were so many, too many, arrows along the way that it was impossible to get lost. At least almost impossible. He did not know that the way had been lost already just an hour before and would most likely be lost again before the way was through. When the road forked, we parted ways and he turned back to wish me *Buen Camino*, the first of many to be heard on the road to Santiago.

Climbing higher, the hills seemed to defy the laws of gravity, always going up and rarely coming down. It was hours before I first caught sight of the sea when the trees gave way, as did the clouds, and the whole of the ocean was revealed under a still rising sun whose light came down in scattered rays upon the coast.

For hours I followed this path as it continued to wind through mountains and towns and snaked along the sea. My steps never slowed, they only quickened in anticipation of what the next turn might bring, which was always a view more breathtaking than the one before. If there was any regret or hesitation for having chosen the more difficult path, it disappeared with the morning mist.

Eventually the road widened, revealing San Sebastian, a city renowned for its beauty and its tapas. The day was still early and the albergue was not to open until the middle of the afternoon so I took my bag and went where I always go when it is summer and there is not a cloud to be found in the sky: the beach. Off came my boots, as did my socks and for hours I dug my toes into the sand and listened as the waves came and went from the shore. Never had I felt more invigorated. Never had I felt more alive.

At half past two the doors to the albergue, a school converted to a hostel for the month of August, opened. In the gymnasium there were rows of bunk beds separated just enough to leave room for bags and boots and little else, but there was a roof overhead and hot coffee for the morning. Nothing more was needed.

Even after a warm shower everything was still in motion: my legs, my head, my heart, my thoughts and so I set out to explore the city. San Sebastian is a petit city of the Pais Basco with a grand promenade and even grander architecture. In the heat of a Spanish summer the streets were full of laughter; everywhere there were celebrations. I imagined that this was the way that Spaniards always live their lives: without a care for anything else. In the windows and on the counters of every bar throughout the city there were pintxos, traditional bite sized snacks that are famous throughout the Pais Basco. Each was different. On one plate were sardines folded in half, a toothpick through the center. On another were croquettes, fried to a golden brown and placed in a pool of rich creamy tomato sauce. There was octopus sautéed only in olive oil and lemon and dressed with fresh parsley and there were also slices of bread stacked high and filled with cured ham and local cheese made from the milk of sheep. It was a food so plenty that it seemed that Spain might be the only place in the world that knew not of hunger.

In want of something sweet to celebrate my first day on the Camino I bought an ice cream cone and ate it as the sun set across the Bay of Biscay. It came down coral, setting the sky on fire as waves peaked and crashed in the shallow sea. Surfers bobbed up and down in the ocean reveling in a summer that was soon to end. When the light all but disappeared, I returned to the albergue where sleep came swiftly and the morning even swifter.

Again, in the darkness I was one of the first to leave. In front of me were three Spaniards and behind walked a French woman with her daughter and for that

171

first week this was our established order as we moved west.

In the approaching dawn I left San Sebastián, passing youth still out from the night before. They leaned into one another as they walked down the promenade with not a care for the years that have passed nor the years that will come. I smiled as I moved through the dispersing crowd, laughing at the memento vita before me. All too aware of a youth that has long since passed I quietly whispered to them: *tu fui ego eris*; "I was once what you are, what I am you will become."

As the sixth hour slowly became the seventh the sky turned a golden pink and the sun crept over the mountains. The wind swept in from the sea, lifting seagulls high into the air, the white of their wings reflecting the dawn. I looked back and watched the world come into the light, knowing that only yesterday I had walked from there to here. It seemed so close and yet so far away. Only nineteen miles had been walked. There were still hundreds of miles to go.

The sun continued to climb, as did I. The coast smelled of citrus and cinnamon, currants and currents, wildflowers and trees whose names I will never know. Wild blackberries ripened under the August sun, rich and plump and purple and just begging to be picked by whoever passed them by. When the city was no more, the way meandered through the orchards and vineyards of the Pais Basco. I wanted to pluck the tiny green and purple pearls of grapes from their vines, but they were not yet ready for harvest. Still summer they would be sour and not sweet. Besides, to do so would make me a thief and in a world that had already given me so much, I thought it best not to take. Hours later I arrived in Zarautz and spent another afternoon laying peacefully in the sand listening to the way the pounding of my heart matched that of the sea.

172

Time passed and I fell into a rhythm of waking and walking where each day was not very different than the one before. In the mornings I snuck out of the albergue to escape from the osos that were still sleeping inside. Competitor and introvert that I am, I loved to be among the first to depart, to emerge into the darkness and to have covered almost three miles before first light. With each sunrise, mountains emerged from the mist and everything was quiet. Climbing each hill my legs ached for more and less at the same time and the heaviness of my breath was balanced by the lightness of my heart. On this solitary route so many hours were spent alone that I began to lose track of them. Like in Goa, time was measured only in the rising and setting of the sun with thousands of steps, like thousands of thoughts between.

Most days the path led through empty towns where neither a car nor a soul was to be seen. The world was asleep. Not that this mattered. I tend not to move in packs and the less people I encountered on this walk, the more I was able to retreat into my own heart; a place I was sometimes afraid to go for fear that I may not like what was found. But still I went.

How else are we to grow if we cannot find the light in the dark?

When the wind came up from the valleys or in from the coast, it rustled the leaves of the eucalyptus trees and brought with it the smell of fresh cut hay that lay on the side of the track in bales wrapped for the fall to come. Each haystack was dry and sweet with a hint of salt from the sea. It was the smell of a fading season; a reminder that even this will not last. As I walked through open fields dotted with round bales of hay, I thought that maybe this is why painters return so often to the places they love the most. To me, to Monet, haystacks are not just haystacks. They are summer. They are the sun.

With another day finished, another beach was found. No longer alone, I went with a Spanish woman named Sarah who was to walk as far as Bilbao before returning to her home in Madrid. Some only complete the trek in stages, walking from one city to another for a week at a time. I wondered if, upon returning to their homes, they longed for the Camino in the way that one longs to finish something that has been left undone. For the rest of the afternoon we lay close to the water, taking turns swimming in the ocean to relieve our tired bodies of the thousands of steps they had taken. Sometimes in Spanish and sometimes in English Sarah and I spoke about lost loves, broken hearts, and future dreams. The tide rose high, the sun sank low and when the day turned to dusk, our thoughts turned to dinner.

In the center of town, we found other hungry pilgrims at a restaurant with room enough for all of us. One by one we went around the table, telling of the reasons why we were here. Somehow, they were all the same. Most on the Camino were there by themselves, carving out a month of their lives to complete this journey. There were Spaniards, Germans, Belgians, and lucky for me, very few Americans. All of us, without exception, were there to go deep, to work hard, to think harder, or not at all. When the conversations turned from heavy to light we laughed about what is it like to sleep among 40 snoring souls, we debated over our preference of going up hills rather than down, and we counted ourselves lucky for so many days without rain, especially in a region known more for its storms than its sun. For dinner, we ate from the pilgrim's menu, which was a three-course meal that included bread and more bottles of wine than could possibly be finished, but we ate and drank it all anyway. There seemed to be so much to celebrate on this Camino with these companions. Small wonder that the word companion simply means one who breaks bread with another. In this way all of us pilgrims are companions, breakers of bread, sharers of life. Before our meal, a pilgrim who sat at the far end of the table offered this as prayer:

"Long tables. Deep glasses. That is all you take from this life."

I repeated this prayer as I thought back on the meals shared throughout this journey and even all of the meals shared before this journey ever began and if I were to measure my life by the length of tables and the depth of glasses, how full and how rich it has always been.

On my fifth day on the Camino I arrived in a town that may have remained unknown to the outside world had it not been for one single day. On April 27, 1937, Nazi forces in support of Spanish dictator Francisco Franco unleashed an aerial bombing upon the civilian population of the city. Guernica is its name. The first of its kind, this assault left sixteen hundred civilians killed or wounded. The city burned for three days. So as to quell the rising dissension against Franco's Nationalist government, it was masterminded and carried out by Hermann Goring as a gift to Adolf Hitler in celebration of his forty-eighth birthday, demonstrating just how cruel the line is between giving and taking. So successful was this air raid in crushing the morale of the inhabitants of Guernica that the same tactics were used on September 1, 1939. The day the blitzkrieg began over Poland.

In the center of Guernica there is a replication of Pablo Picasso's painting of the same name, which depicts the gruesomeness of war, the cruelty of man, and the atrocities that unfolded here on that spring day. It is a mural drained of color, drained of life. It is said that years later, when the Germans occupied Paris, a Nazi officer visited the studio of Picasso. He stood in front of a photograph of this painting and asked Picasso, "Did you do that?" "No," Picasso replied, "you did." To this day, Guernica remains one of the loudest cries against war.

I stood in front of this painting until all of the light left the day, all too aware that if Picasso were to paint this brutal scene of war now, almost a century later, nothing in this composition would change, for nothing in the world has changed, except perhaps that war has become more brutal, more vicious, more precise, and just far enough away from the West that we can pretend that these wars do not take place at all. When it was still dark, I left Guernica with these thoughts exploding like bombs in my head.

From then on, all cities were skipped. Enough days had been spent in them in the past four months that the thought of staying another night among millions after having walked alone for hours was unthinkable, which is why, after having arrived in Bilbao so early in the morning, I continued west, all the way to Pobena, the amount of kilometers forgotten under the late summer sun. By the time I arrived, the albergue was full and there was nowhere to sleep but outside. And so, I slept

176

underneath a single streetlight with the waves of the not so distant sea as my lullaby, praying for once that it would not rain

Days became weeks on the Camino. Two hundred and fifty miles had been walked and there was still two hundred and fifty more to go. But the miles mattered less now for every step had become not a step forward, but a step inward to the places I could no longer and would no longer hide. The haj of my heart, the jihad of my soul had begun.

The most difficult day on the Camino came somewhere in the middle when I arrived in an industrial town thinking that more than enough miles had been walked for the day, but there was still so many more to go. When the sun escaped from behind the clouds the day grew hotter. Everywhere there was noise. A pipeline lay parallel to the path. It wound from one end of the city to the other, humming and buzzing, a constant static, an interrupted peace. Even when the limits of the city were reached there was no shade, there was not even wind. There was nothing but empty roads, empty cornfields, and an empty sky. Minutes felt like hours. Hours felt like an eternity. With each step I slowed, not wanting to take another.

A train or a bus could have been taken to avoid all of this and not let it "ruin" my Camino, but then I remembered that not all days were meant to be beautiful. Some were noisy and loud and dirty and messy, and I was left with no other choice but to walk through them because this was my choice. I chose to walk the Camino.

177

And in the awareness of what a privilege this choice was, I wept. I wept for how bearable my pain was compared to the pain of others. I wept because there is no comparison. I wept for all of the refugees who I had shared the road with who would have given anything to walk with freedom and not fear; to have been the ones to have made this choice rather than have this choice made for them. I wept for everything that has ever been lost: a life, a love, a country. There is no comparison. So distraught was I that I took off my backpack that seemed to hold the weight of the world and laid down on the side of the road where I cried with an ache so deep that I feared I might never return to the surface, but to drown was to forget the reasons for this journey and for those reasons I kept on going.

Early in the afternoon, bruised and battered, I entered the medieval city of Santillana del Mar, The Town of Three Lies. It is called so because despite the implications of its name it is neither a Saint, nor flat, nor is it by the sea. Although only 17.7 kilometers had been walked, it felt as if I had walked the entire coast and for what remained of the day, I lay in the shade of a sycamore tree still lost in the thoughts of the afternoon.

From Santillana del Mar, there were fewer pilgrims, the albergues grew smaller and the road grew quiet. The last days of August were marked by mornings shrouded in mist and the darkness of an earlier dusk. Soon this summer would end. Already, autumn was longing to begin.

For five months there were so few days filled with rain that after the first month I counted all the days without. Eighty-six days. Almost three months without rain and even after the rain in Serbia it had not rained again. But at the end of August, there was talk of rain. Not a passing storm but a tempest that would rage for hours, perhaps even days. In the gloaming I stood on top of a hill in the small town of San Martin de Laspra and watched the sun sink behind the mountains, waiting for the rain.

With the dawn, clouds, steel and gray, gathered in the hills, stripping the sun of its light and the heat from the day. After the first kilometer it began to drizzle, then came the wind, and then the flood. It came down hard, splashing against the concrete and creating puddles everywhere. This was the rain that I had been waiting for over one hundred days. For hours it rained mercy and it rained grace and for the first time on the Camino I stood still and let it wash over me. This rain was my ablution, my blessing, my baptism, and in its deluge, I was free. As the sky opened, I too opened my arms to its torrent, welcoming each drop as it fell and shouting into the sky the only two words that mattered on this journey:

THANK YOU.

I said it first in English and then in Spanish, French, Italian, Turkish, and finally in Arabic for good measure. I said it in every language learned on this pilgrimage. *Gracias. Merci. Grazie. Hvala vam. Teşekkürler. Shukran.* For this I was grateful. For this I gave thanks.

Somewhere between San Martin de Laspra and Soto de Luina I stopped at the sea and watched the water churn and crash against the rocks. The shore was made of stones in shades of ash and smoke. I picked a small flat stone up, turning it over in my hands before skipping

179

it into the ocean, counting the number of times it skimmed the surface before sinking into the darkened waters. As it sunk, I made a wish and a promise to remember this day to forever. How could I not? It was Wednesday, August 30, 2017; my thirty-seventh birthday.

I arrived at the albergue soaked from head to toe, my waterproof boots full of water, not a dry stitch on my shorts, and still a smile on my face. After exchanging wet clothes for dry I walked into town to drink a beer, straight from the bottle, trying to remember a more perfect birthday but it was impossible. Never has there been such a day. When night came, crowding the day with its darkness, I fell asleep, another year older, another step closer to Santiago.

The next morning the sun rised and shined as if it thought nothing of the past and had already forgotten the day before.

You cannot fault the sun. It knows nothing of night or rain or darkness. It knows only light.

Not long from the dawn clouds still covered the coast and the wind still carried with it a hint of rain. I sat on a beach watching the sea after the storm. It was restless, rising over the rocks covering them with salt and foam. Looking back, I saw him before he saw me. He came down the hill with fire and fury. His name was Kevin, although I did not know it at the time but soon would learn. From a distance I thought that perhaps he was yet another German, with hair so blond that it seemed white and eyes that looked no different than the sky after the rain. But he was not. He was from Estonia. His accent was almost implacable, having learned English from watching American films and living in Australia. He walked with a stick he had found in some town before carved with pagan symbols that reminded him of the Viking he wished to be. In his hands he held a camera and he had climbed to the edge of a cliff to capture the last of the coast. He told me that he had taken so many photographs since Irun that they all began to look the same. I knew not what he meant. So enamored had I become with photography, so in love with light, that the thousands of pictures, like the thousands of steps I had taken, did not seem to be enough. He was gone before that thought was finished, disappearing into the woods almost as quickly as he had appeared, and I wondered if it was all just a dream.

That day, I stopped after only twelve miles. Those twelve were enough. I was the first at the albergue. Only moments later did Pablo arrive, a twenty-three-year-old Spaniard from Santiago. His eyes lit up like stars when he spoke and even when he was only smiling, you could hear the laughter in his voice. He wore his long hair in a bun on top of his head and his beard looked like it hadn't been trimmed in days, maybe even weeks, but it suited him, this beautiful disarray. After putting down his bag he took down his hair that fell in waves upon his handsome face. I loved him from the moment we met. I loved the ease of his smile, his joy and his sadness, and the way he said everything without saying anything at all. This was his second Camino of the summer. In July he had walked the French way. He had already walked 831 kilometers and now he was here to walk some more. Perhaps he was young enough to believe that he could outrun his demons and not old enough to know that such a thing was impossible. We spoke for most of the afternoon and even some of the night about everything and about nothing and I knew by morning that no matter how far the distance, no matter how long the time, we would always be friends. Always.

With Pablo began three days of walking more than thirty kilometers a day. He had lost his friends and

181

was determined to find them again and I wanted to evade once and for all a determined Spaniard that only knew how to speak small.

On the first of September an early escape was made from the albergue, the Milky Way visible in the sky above. It spread from one end of the night to the other offering its stars as guides. I followed it for miles until the sun swept the stars away with its light, leaving only one for the day.

Every day on this journey I was made all too aware of the burdens that I carried in my heart and on my back. For years I had allowed unimportant things to weigh me down, thinking that it was this weight that made me stronger when just the opposite is true. After miles, ounces felt like pounds. There was so little in my pack that was needed anymore. Gone went the mascara and out went the dress that was no longer being saved for a special occasion. I may have even torn out pages from books that had already been read just to lighten the load. But I was not the only one leaving things behind. Along the Camino there are piles of rocks that pilgrims have carried with them on this journey. Often referred to as Stones of Burden, they are meant to honor the loves in our lives that have been lost or as a plea for forgiveness for the mistakes that we might have made. Whenever they are ready, pilgrims place these small stones down to ease their hearts of these burdens. I, too, left my stone on the Camino, hopefully never to be picked up again. It took until mountains to realize that up until now I had only been carrying around pebbles and not the heavy stones they sometimes seemed. It took until the sea to learn that some things are meant to be left behind.

After another day of walking over hills and through valleys I arrived in Arzua. Pablo was there. Along the way, he had met Amina, a Moroccan woman who now lives in Germany. She reminded me of my

182

aunts, Anna and Anita, with her wild hair and her wild thoughts. Together we cooked dinner and talked late into the night. Like others on the Camino, they, too, were here for the same reason: to seek out whom they were when no one else was watching. As Amina poured a glass of wine and Pablo rolled cigarettes, we spoke of our families and things we did not understand. Although our differences were many, our stories were very much the same. Through our varied interpretations we all saw ourselves as the black sheep in our families, the ones who marched to the beat of their own drums. It was Pablo who saw to the heart of it:

"Yes, I am different, but I am really good at being different."

We recounted our journeys thus far, not just on the Camino, but also in life. Together we decided that if you were not emotionally attached to the steps that you are taking you would not get very far. Our conversation turned to vulnerability and despite the difficulties that we faced on the Camino; Amina admitted:

"I don't want to be a rock. I want to be soft, not hard." Her words were few but easily understood. After all, we are made of water. We are not made of stone. We stayed up past midnight, whispering in the dark until sleep came for us. We said goodnight with hopes of finding one another somewhere down the road.

The sun rose slowly over the Asturian coast, the clouds changing from deep purple to bright pink and the ocean always blue. The hills grew smaller and the road grew flatter and the landscape was brazened with hydrangea: periwinkle blue, pink, lavender and white. Soon the path would turn from the sea, but for now I could still feel the salt against my skin and the freedom of the wind across the water.

The hours of the day passed slowly. By the twenty-seventh kilometer my stride grew small and my

183

legs grew heavy. Descending the last of the hills in zigzags, my toes found the front of my boots and my knees buckled at the thought of another step and so I collapsed on the last of the sandy beaches. I was tired of walking, tired of moving, tired of thinking. That night I did not care if this was the place that I was to sleep. I could walk no more. I lay on the sand until the sun began to fall and the wind stole the warmth from the day. Then I continued. On the edge of the beach there was a rock, standing out among all others, upon which was etched:

"La cura para todo esta en algun salada; lagrimas, sudor e el mar."

Long ago, I had committed this quote by Isak Dinesen to memory in English and was now reminded of it again in Spanish.

"The cure for anything is saltwater: sweat, tears or the sea."

Walking away, barefoot and bereft, I thought that maybe asking to be cured by salt is too much, but I never knew a tear, a bead of sweat, or a drop in the ocean to be anything short of beautiful and here on the Camino was found all three.

Knowing that there might not be a bed that night, I arrived at the small hotel anyway and told what was already known to be true. With the sun fading as quickly as I was, I walked onward ready to sleep outside again, but no more than a kilometer was walked when the young man from the hotel drove to find me saying there had been a cancellation and that there was indeed room for me. I counted my blessings again, this time on more than just my fingers and toes, although by now I knew that even if I counted to infinity it would still not be high enough.

The light came later now and by the time the sun rose over the trees, the ocean was far from view. I found Pablo on top of the first hill and together we walked the first hours of the day. When we stopped for coffee at a small café in a village surrounded by mountains, we were joined by Michael, an Israeli who now lived in Germany. Hypocrite that I am, I asked him what he thought of his country. He was silent for a moment before he answered:

"Give me a few drinks and then we will speak about it." I wanted to ask him to speak about it now, for I have learned that if you cannot speak about something sober, it is best not to speak about it at all. But I did not. That was the first and last time that I brought it up and to this day I am ashamed of my silence for it is silence that shows complicity more so than any words that could ever be spoken. To make light of so heavy a conversation we moved on to telling dirty jokes, always the safest way out of sorrow. What privilege distance affords us. We moved inland, towards Lourenza, our first city far from the coast. By then, Pablo had found his friends, all seven of them. Now there were two Italians, Francesco and Leti, a German, Kim, a Moroccan, a Pole, Dajana, an Israeli, Kevin the Estonian, Pablo, and me the only way I like myself: the lone American. We were a motley crew of pilgrims on their way to Santiago.

Late in the summer the sun became lazy and the days lost their edge. Sometimes, in the cool of the morning, my breath could be seen, crystalizing in the air before disappearing into the dawn. Once in Galicia everything shifted: the light, the trees, the landscape and it felt as if walking in a dream of brume and fog as the way slowly transformed from highway to road, road into lane, and lane into wooded path and then into mist.

Before the road widened and the crowds loomed larger, I was overcome by a sadness that I had not yet a place for. Perhaps it was regret for not having stood still longer, spoken softer, walked slower. Perhaps I was not ready for this journey to end. But still I moved forward, a word from Old English, meaning toward the future even though here, on this walk, I was so unbelievably present.

There were few days left on the Camino. More than 375 kilometers had been walked. Only 167 kilometers remained. Each day Santiago grew closer and each day we wanted it to be further away. Most of this last week was spent with just Pablo and Kevin; three loners that had somehow found one another on the Camino. Sometimes during the day, but mostly at night, we found one another to share our hopes and our fears, our secrets and our sorrows. For those last few days they were the ones that I wanted beside me. With them I felt joy. With them I felt peace.

On our last day on the Camino we stopped at the house of Pablo's grandmother, who lives on the road to Santiago. It was just Pablo, Kevin, and I. The rest were behind us for they view crowds differently than the three of us: They welcome. We scorn. Away from the crowds it was quiet. There, there would be noise. Here we could pretend, at least for a little while, that we were the only ones in the world. There, we would be reminded that we were not. Once inside her home she fed us from wheels of hard cheese and figs just picked from the trees in her garden, their skins purple and plump, their flesh soft and

186

in their ripening the awareness that not all is meant to last. We stayed for no more than an hour, even though none of us were ready to leave. It was then that we knew that our Camino, the one without crowds, had already ended just days before. But Santiago was less than fifteen kilometers away. To stop now would be silly. At her gate the three of us parted ways and we walked alone for the last of it.

And finally, Santiago.

From the top of the last hill I caught sight of the spires rising above the terra cotta roofs of the city. The steeples came and went from view as the way meandered through the streets of Santiago. And then there was no escaping it. After walking over five hundred miles there it was: The Cathedral of Santiago de Compostela. For the last time on the Camino, I dropped my bag and kicked off my boots and yet I could not wipe the tears from my eyes or the grin from my face.

Amina was already in Santiago. I found her in the courtyard standing in awe of the cathedral and her accomplishment. She had arrived the day before and together we toasted to our journeys with bottles of Grenacha and Tempranillo. We drank straight from the lip, taking deep sips of the crimson liquid, letting it stain our teeth and linger on our lips for there was no other way to celebrate such a feat. I waited for all of them, knowing what I have done, they, too, have done. Francesco arrived next. He walked through the square with his arms opened wide and a smile even wider. Next came Pablo, then Kevin, and finally the rest. Together we stared up at the bell towers. The façade was under construction and I could help but think how this church was no different than any of us: a work in progress, a project incomplete.

187

The hostel where we stayed for one last night together was not far from the cathedral. While they napped, I showered, shaved my legs, put on a dress, and went to find a quiet place to remember these past five months of following a path of war and somehow finding peace. There, I raised a glass to myself: a gin martini straight up with a twist. It was a humble celebration, a toast to a small victory and a journey never ending. Again, I called my mother and cried; she cried too. Again, I was happy.

It was just the three of us now. Pablo, Kevin and I. Leti had gone back to Italy, Dajana to Barcelona, and Francesco, Michael, and Kim had gone on to Finisterre, but I know that if it was the ends of the world that needed to be reached, it is these boys who I would reach it with; with them I would go to the depths of hell.

Two days later, we waited in line for our certificates. When our time had come, we told of all the miles that had been walked before receiving a stamp and a smile in return. To them we were just one of the 278,232 pilgrims that will pass this way this year alone. But for that day, it was just us.

After, in between the rain and the sun, we ate *pulpo, pepitos*, and *pollo* and drank *cervezas* to celebrate how far we had come and how far we had yet to go. We spent the rest of the afternoon at Pablo's apartment until it was time for me to leave. I hugged them goodbye. Three times each. These boys are my brothers, my companions, my heart. I missed them before I even left them, not knowing when I might see either of them again, but still I held them as close as I could, afraid as always to let go.

Early in the evening I got on a bus bound for the airport. Out the window I watched as the bus retraced the steps that were taken to arrive in Santiago only days before: yellow arrows, all in a row, where will they lead next? When it came time to relieve my bag of even more weight, I found a rock, a small shale stone, placed there on purpose by Pablo. On one side of the flat surface he had written:

U are the light in the dark.

On the other:

U gived me the wings.

I cried as I clasped it in my hands, near to my heart, keeping it there on my flight from Spain to England and onward from England to America. Now it sits on my nightstand, reminding me of what it means to fly.

A JOURNEY
WITHOUT END

I used to have a hollow heart; a heart so hollow that when storms came, rather than welcoming them, my heart became the storm itself. With each tempest it filled with thunder, it filled with lightening, and it filled with fury. A heart that when it beat it echoed the heavens and it echoed hell. And when the seasons changed, so did my heart, welcoming the snows of winter, the rains of spring, the suns of summer, and the falling of autumn, calling them its own. Now this heart that was so hollow is everything but. And it is not only my heart that is full. All of me is full, of memories; too many to hold in one place.

My ears they echo songs of joy, of prayer, and of silence.
My hands still hold tightly all that they have held in their grasp: the hands of a lover, a stranger, a refugee.
My feet remember the ways they have walked.
My face remembers the kiss of the wind.
My skin, the sun.
My eyes, everything.

I will remember all of it.
I will forget nothing.

For my heart is not empty.

My heart is full.

The poems

If I Were King

If I were king
I, too, would build a fort
At the top of a hill
So very different from the forts of my childhood
Made only with pillows and blankets
And the innocence of youth
Unbound by fears of invasion

If I were king
I, too, would paint my palace pink
And play endless games of hide and go seek,
go seek, go seek
With monkeys, with elephants
As I have done thousands of times before
in my imagination

But now alone
With neither palace nor primate to call my own
I still declare myself king:
Sultan of refuge
Maharajah of the mountains
For now I am sovereign only to one.
And so for today I am king.

Today I am king.

197

An Afternoon in Lodhi Gardens

Somewhere between
that which is old
and that which is new
there is a garden that sprawls
centuries and civilizations

Seeking shelter from a relentless sun
I sit in the shadow of a neem
Lost in the comparison
of trees and tombs

Wondering which of these speaks of life
and which speaks of death
Unable to separate the two
a breeze lifts
carrying with it both the sounds of the city
and the songs of birds
who have but little use
for all that remains on the ground

And then the realization
These boughs will break
These walls will fall
There is nothing to compare
They are one and the same

199

Morning in Varanasi

I am awake
cautious of each step taken in the darkness
For it is not only papers,
yesterday's news,
that scatter the streets.

The barking of dogs,
the honking of horns,
a procession of priests:
How easily men sleep through it all.
And then the river.

From its ancient banks
bells call out to Venus
still visible in the distance
and holy men,
clad in robes so orange,
making you wonder if they are the rising sun.

Far from the ghat
a man turns his back from the swelling crowd.
Facing east, he plays the flute.
He is a charmer of the sun,
asking one star to give way to another.
Silently I listen
and wait for the light to come.

Cedars of the Gods

I do not know much about cedars.
I do not know their Latin name.
I do not know from which class they come or what order
they fall into.
I do not know why some of these cedars were chosen for
more fleeting fates
while others still stand as they have stood for thousands of
years
and will continue to stand for thousands of years more.

But I do know how easily the light of the sun penetrates
through the canopy of their branches
and the coolness of their shade.
I know how the colors and the shape of their bodies
change, like ours, with the passing of time
from the brown thickness of youth
to the gray thinness of age.
I know the way the wind feels as it moves through these
trees and down the valley
on an afternoon in May
and how small the mountains seem now that they are
close enough to touch.

And while this is all I know of cedars; this seems to be
enough.

202

Breathe

I do not know when it was
that I lost my ability to breath.
Was it when I first caught sight of metal
twisted into the shapes of barrels, stocks and triggers? Or
when I walked across a desert
that showed no sign of promise
and no sign of mercy?
Or was it when I stood with my mother
in front of this gate
for hours
waiting for a bus that never came?

I suppose losing your freedom feels the same;

like being unable to breathe.

To Stand in Grace

If this is the day that death comes for me
I will tell him that I am ready
For now I know what it feels like
to share coffee with a stranger.
I know the feel of the sun in the morning
on one side of the world
and in the afternoon on the other.

I know the feel of the sea as,
in the parting of its waters,
it is sprayed
like prayers,
like hope,
like peace,
into the air

and how many shades
of turquoise that there really are.

And I know what it is like to stand in awe
of a place centuries older than my oldest dreams;
to feel the coolness of its marble,
the warmth of its light,

I know what it is like to witness the intricacies
of its mosaics,
its latticework,
its brocades.
I know with what intimacy its calligraphy was traced.

I now know what it is like to stand in grace.

And because of all of this,
when death comes for me,
as he comes for us all,
perhaps not on this day,
but one day all too soon,

I will tell him that now,
now I am ready.

For I have stood in grace.

Years later will I be able to recall these days?
Will I be able to recall
The ache of the wind that brought with at the ancient
longing
Of an ancient forest?

The way that mountains appeared and disappeared
behind clouds and from one another?

The rain that fell on the roof
The bright heat of the sun
The absence of the moon
The rush of the river at night
All of those wildflowers.

I don't know if I will.
But then again, how can I possibly forget all of those
stars?

211

Eighty-Six Days

It has been eighty-six days without rain.
Eighty- six days
of heat without mercy
and sun without solace.
But when the rains fall
from the mountains into this valley,
they make no apologies for their absence
nor will they apologize
for the abruptness of their departure.

And the skies,
so empty for so long,
must now find their fill
with clouds,
with wonder,
and with woe

And I remember just how much I miss thunder,
how much I miss lightening,
how much I miss this,
and just how long I have been waiting for these rains to
fall.

The Death of Trees

Come with me.
I want to share with you the story
of the death of trees.

Somewhere between standing and falling they rock
back and forth,
their boughs browned,
their limbs leafless,
breaking the silence of the world
with their sighs and their sorrows.

In fear of their own height
and the nearness of the ground below
they ask of the wind the impossible:
To slow. To cease.

To which the wind answers,
its voice hushed,
its touch tender:

Come.
It is time.
When you fall,
in my arms you will be caught
and I will take you with me.

214

Come with me
and I will tell you
The story of life.

At the Atelier of Paul Cezanne

In this room fruit is still kept on the table.
It has begun to whither and weather,
as have the ceilings,
which are cracked and beiged
and the walls of slate that I imagine turn blue
at certain times of the day.

The floors creak under the weight of visitors who gather
around:
A box of paints,
their colors faded and hardened by the toll of years.

A bottle of wine that holds one hundred years
of sediments of crimson and ash at its bottom.
A collection of umbrellas in the corner;
Which one was used,
if any, on that fateful day?

A candle stands unilluminated for a century.
Above, rosaries for praying hang from a shelf.

Below, skulls for reminding just how futile those prayers
may be.

217

From beyond the window
the sun breaks free from clouds
flooding the studio with light,
flooding the studio with life

But it is only temporary before these moments of stillness
arrive once again.

These moments of death.

A breeze enters;
rustling the leaves on the trees,
which, like the fruit on the table,
have already begun to brown.

But, even in the twilight they still blush, embarrassed as
they are to have exchanged their colors of summer for
those of autumn so soon.

But they know,
Just as I know that this fruit,
these leaves,
this August will not last.
Only this room will.

It is as he left it.
He was here.

He is here still.

218

When I wake at three, I do not try to fall back asleep.
Jet lagged; my body knows not where it is.
As to remind myself of where I now stand
I return to the north of a once far away land.
I turn to the east.
But it does not work.
My feet remember the sand of other shores,
my skin remembers the salt of other seas,
and my heart remembers all of it:
The wind and the wildflowers
The stars and the sun
The sounds and the silence
that will forever echo across the waters of my soul,
which is why my heart is still in all of those places and not
here, not yet.

In Istanbul
it had been sixty-nine days
without rain.
And now as I sit and listen
to the cold rain
fall hard on the roof
I count back from January to July
and realize it has been
one hundred and ninety-five days
without Istanbul
and just how much Istanbul
for me
was like rain.
Like love.
Like life.
And how, even now, over half a year later,
when I close my eyes
and listen to this call to prayer
it is as if I am still there,
for it is only my feet that have left.
All else remained
in this city of my heart.

List of Figures

*All photographs have been taken by the author, Briana Gervat, with an iPhone 6s.

ACKNOWLEDGMENTS

My heart is a hopeful thing; how it skips and somersaults as it remembers this pilgrimage.

There was not a day that went by that I was not reminded by my mother or my best friend that not only is it that what you seek you will find, but also that you get what you come for. But I would never have gotten very far if it were not for them and all the people I met on this journey. They number so many and my gratitude for them is so great that I will spend the rest of my life indebted to the embrace that this world offered me.

I went away with the hope that I might finally understand war, life, myself. Maybe I understand all of it a little bit more. Maybe I understand all of it a little bit less. Or maybe, just maybe, I am still somewhere in between.

Now back from the far side of the world, I feel as if it were all a mirage, but a mirage in which I still find peace like a desert. In search of my softer self I found the softness in others too. And while I witnessed things that I will always find difficult to understand or even accept, there are things that must always be accepted: coffee in the morning, cay in the afternoon, a smile between strangers, the breaking of bread, a wink, a nod of the head. For a kindness is a kindness no matter where you

226

are in the world.

To this day this journey reverberates through my soul and within these pages I tried my best to put to words what was seen, what was felt and what was heard from beginning to end. Some words may have been forgotten, while others echo across each chapter, reiterating the many themes of this book: that this world is good, that people are kind, and that there is, above all, hope.

I wish to thank everyone whose path I crossed on this journey and while our paths may never again meet, know that my feet still feel lucky to have fallen in step with your own.

Until then, we walk on.

A Prayer for Saint Veronica, the Patron Saint of
Photography.

O my Jesus, Saint Veronica served you on the way to
Cavalry by wiping your beloved face with a towel on
which your sacred image then appeared. She protected
this treasure and whenever people touched it there were
miraculously healed. I ask her to pray for the growth of
my ability to see your sacred images in others, to
recognize their hurts, to stop and join them on their
difficult journeys and to feel the same compassion for
them as she did you. Show me how to wipe their faces,
serve their needs, heal their wounds, reminding me that
as I do this for them, I also do this for you.

Saint Veronica, pray for me. Amen.

Made in the USA
Middletown, DE
16 February 2020

84867080R00144